Sibling Stories

Reflections on Life with a Brother or Sister on the Autism Spectrum

Lynne Stern Feiges, Esq.
Mary Jane Weiss, Ph.D./BCBA

Preface by Sandra L. Harris, Co-author
Siblings of Children with Autism – A Guide for Families

APC

Autism Asperger Publishing Co.
P.O. Box 23173
Shawnee Mission, KS 66283-0173

©2004 Autism Asperger Publishing Co.
P.O. Box 23173
Shawnee Mission, KS 66283-0173
www.asperger.net

Publisher's Cataloging-in-Publication
(Provided by Quality Books, Inc.)

Feiges, Lynne Stern.
    Sibling stories : reflections on life with a brother
or sister on the Autism spectrum / Lynne Stern Feiges
and Mary Jane Weiss ; preface by Sandra L. Harris

    p. cm.
    Includes bibliographical references.
    Library of Congress Control Number: 2004101469
    ISBN 1-931282-54-4

    1. Autistic children–Family relationships.
2. Asperger's syndrome–Patients–Family relationships.
3. Brothers and sisters–Family relationships. 4. Brothers
and sisters–Mental health. 5. Family. I. Weiss,
Mary Jane. II Title.

RJ506.A9F45 2004   618.92'8982
                               QBI33-1726

This book is designed in Papyrus and Gill Sans

Managing Editor: Kirsten McBride
Cover Design: Vivian Strand

Printed in the United States of America

Dedication

for Lauren, Liam, and Nora

and

for Rich

Acknowledgments

Mary Jane Weiss is grateful to Sandra Harris, for teaching her about the complexities of autism and of families, and for her wisdom, guidance, humor, and friendship over the past 20 years. She also thanks Jan Handleman, for his mentorship and support, and her wonderful colleagues at the Douglass Developmental Disabilities Center – especially Lara Delmolino, Beth Glasberg, Jacqueline Wright, Maria Arnold, Barbara Kristoff, Rita Gordon, Marlene Brown, Marlene Cohen, and Donna Sloan – for the camaraderie and support day in and day out. A sincere thank you goes to all the people with autism and all of the families of people with autism that Mary Jane has been privileged to get to know over the years – thank you for all you have taught me about autism, about families, and about love.

Mary Jane is personally grateful to her parents; her loving father, the late William Coneys, who embodied both strength and gentleness, and her mother, Joan Rita Coneys, her true heroine, who is a model of compassion and of strength, and who blesses her with limitless love and loyalty. She thanks her aunt, Veronica McSweeney, who showers her with love and devotion, and who encourages her in all endeavors. She thanks her siblings, Ruth Anne Guerrero and the late William Coneys, who taught her more than anyone else about life and about the power of love. She also appreciates the joy provided by her nieces Lisa and Jessica. Gratitude also goes to the Weiss family: Pearl, Gerry, Jennifer, David, Andrea, and Jake: thanks for being another wonderful family to belong to. Mary Jane also thanks her family of friends, especially Ellen Yeagle, Jacqueline Geoghegan, and Lisa Martin for being there, and Geno Alfonzo for keeping everyone (including me) happy. A special thank you goes to co-author and forever friend, Lynne, who was a great task master and a fabulous friend throughout this project, and who is a constant source of inspiration and joy. Finally, Mary Jane thanks Liam and Nora, for being the blessings and joys that they are to her and to each other, and Danny, for everything and for always.

Lynne Stern Feiges thanks her family: Her incredible husband, Greg, for being her "rock," for making her laugh every day, and, most important, for fixing her computer when it exploded two minutes before a deadline; her daughter, Lauren, the "minister of happiness" and clearly the best thing that ever happened; Len and Ceil Stern, the strongest and loyalest parents of them all; Michael, Paula, Joey, and Bella Stern, for Michael's honesty and crazy humor, and for all the good times; Seth Stern, for always trying so hard; Richard Stern, for being the mighty "Riz," remaining so dear and teaching everyone a thing or two about life; and Bev, Lew, Brian, and Howard Feiges, for their support and for all our great adventures together.

Lynne is also grateful for her golden friendship with Nancy Ciardullo, who has always had a special place in Rich's heart. And, huge thanks go to her wonderful ATLA colleagues, past and present, who taught her so much over the years. Additionally, she thanks other close friends who provided constant support and inspiration: Carol Deaktor, Deb Meisel, Sarah Barrett, Carla Bauman-Schenck, Lisa Deverey, Jodi Moraru, Jonathan and Suzanne Seigel, and the late Kevin McQuarrie.

Lastly, Lynne thanks Mary Jane, for always having such incredible (and always hilarious) insight about just about everything, and for making this project so fulfilling. Your friendship is a rare and true gift.

Lynne and Mary Jane both thank Sandra Harris, for her enthusiasm and belief in the importance of this project, as well as for her encouragement along the way. They also thank Herb Hinkle, Esq., for his review of Appendix A. Many thanks also go to Kirsten McBride, for her sharp editorial eye and dedication to making this manuscript the best it could possibly be. Thanks are also extended to the families who shared their photos.

Finally, and deeply, Lynne and Mary Jane thank the siblings who opened their hearts to them. Your moving stories will serve as a beacon of hope to others.

Table of Contents

Preface

Parents of children, adolescents and adults with autism often share with me their concerns about the impact on their other children of growing up in a household that includes a child with autism. How can they buffer their children from the negative effects of having a brother or sister whose behavior is so problematic? Will there be enduring psychological harm? What role does a sibling play in caring for a child with autism? What are a sibling's responsibilities for an adult brother or sister with autism? Siblings too have described to me their experiences with a sibling with autism and often said they wonder if what happened to them growing up was unusual, or whether other people share the same reactions to their brother or sister with autism. They grapple with questions such as, "Why did he get autism and not me," "Do I risk having a child with autism," and "What is my role for him after my parents die?"

These kinds of important questions reflect all parents' concern for the welfare of each of their children, and the nearly universal parental wish to do the best they can to support their child's development. They also reflect the enduring need of most of us to make sense of what we experience and to find a community in which we can address our concerns. Sometimes a book can be part of such a community.

Lynne Stern Feiges and Mary Jane Weiss have written a highly engaging and very useful book about what it means to be the brother or sister of a person with autism. Through their interviews with siblings across the age span, they have been granted a window into the lives of people who grew up with a bother or sister on the autism spectrum. What they learned and have put into this book will enrich the lives of siblings and parents alike.

Both authors bring to the writing of this book their scholarship and the fundamental experiences of their own lives. Lynne is herself the sister of a man with autism and Mary Jane grew up with a brother who had a chronic medical illness. Both authors know first-hand what it is like to be helpless in the face of a sibling's needs, and they both know how it felt to sometimes have to step aside to make room for the needs of a brother with serious problems. Very significantly, both grew up to be compassionate women who feel a duty to speak on behalf of others who lack a voice. Mary Jane is a clinical psychologist and board certified behavior analyst who serves people with autism and their families, trains others in this work, and writes and lectures extensively on the treatment of autism. Lynne is an attorney and writer who has focused her career on issues related to mental health and victims' rights.

The authors are also role models for other siblings of how one can cope with the challenges of life with a brother or sister who has autism or another serious disability, and emerge in adulthood as a productive, caring person who lives a rich, full life. Both have remained involved with their families of origin, advocating for their siblings and supporting their parents, and both have established their own loving families as well.

The voices of the siblings who were interviewed for this book speak eloquently to how one can experience the full gamut of tender and painful feelings, address the special demands of living with a sibling with autism, and grow richer and stronger in one's compassion, wisdom and life experience. Living with autism is a challenge, but it is not a catastrophe. Far from it, as these participants reveal, siblings of people with significant disabilities can master the challenges that come their way and through that experience of mastery be prepared for the many complex demands that are part of every person's life.

Sandra Lee Harris, Ph.D.
Professor, and Board of Governors
Distinguished Service Professor
Rutgers, The State University
Winter 2004

Introduction

Like so many things in life, this book was born out of strong links between people. In the early 1970s, my parents began their search for answers regarding my 5-year-old brother Richard's condition. They had been told so many painful untruths about his problems, including that they were caused by my mother's supposed "coldness" toward him and that he suffered from schizophrenia that necessitated lifelong institutionalization. Never ones to go down without a fight, my parents continued looking for the right treatment for Rich.

During this process they were lucky enough to meet Dr. Sandra L. Harris, then a professor at Rutgers University and a founder of the Douglass Developmental Disabilities Center (DDDC). She led them to another nearby program for young people with autism, which went on to serve Richard in its school and group home for the next 25 years.

My family was stable and happy during these years, but I still had feelings and questions about autism that I didn't necessarily share, even with my older typically developing brother with whom I had a close relationship. While studying at Rutgers in the mid-1980s, I decided to see what I could learn by working with other people with autism. This brought me to the fieldwork program at DDDC, where I heard lectures by Sandy and others about current treatment methods (some of which I had been seeing for years) and where I became eventual friends with my teacher Mary Jane. She and I remained great friends after graduation and, even though we didn't talk about autism all that much, it was always comforting for me to know that someone I liked and respected so much was contributing to the field that impacted me and my family so significantly.

Years later, I had another chance meeting, this time with an energetic couple whose toddler was receiving services from Mary Jane after being diagnosed with an autism spectrum disorder (ASD). The couple described their struggle to me and their quest to find the best help possible for their son. After listening for a while, I told them that my brother had autism and had lived for many years at a group home. Almost immediately, the conversation turned to the issue of the couple's typically developing child. They confided in me that they felt she was not getting enough attention and asked what they could do to protect her feelings and her needs. Although I wanted to provide some advice, I could not find the words to adequately express myself. I had not yet sorted these issues out for myself.

After this encounter, it became clear to Mary Jane and to me that other people might be curious about what it is like to have a sibling with ASD. To try to come to grips with this, we began contacting adults and children who have journeyed through life with such a brother or sister. In some cases, we accessed siblings through advertisements in local advocacy group newsletters. In other instances, we met siblings through Internet sibling support groups or through personal contacts. The people we interviewed – in person, over the telephone, and through their written correspondence – were from all over the country. They also were of different ages and came from families with diverse structures, functionality, and living arrangements.

Almost without exception, we found a profound need on the siblings' part to share their stories and trade information on coping with the impact of ASD in their family. We were greatly moved by what the siblings had to say, and the interviews confirmed what the research tells us: That siblings of people with ASD face daunting emotional and practical challenges that change over the life span of the sibling relationship.

Sibling Stories is a collection of these honest and inspirational interviews organized under several themes – overlapping at times – that emerged from our conversations. Interestingly, the siblings we spoke to shared some, but not all, of the same struggles and triumphs, largely depending on the circumstances each family faced. To reflect this, we have separated the book into sections. Chapter 1 is an introductory chapter discussing sibling relationships and introducing the siblings included in this book. Chapters 2 through 5 center on the themes of (a) family effects, (b) responsibility, (c) emotional impact and interpersonal effects, and (d) positive aspects, respectively. Chapter 6 focuses on coping strategies for managing the effects of ASD. This format, we hope, will allow readers to access the themes they find most important to them.

Within Chapters 2 through 5, we have grouped verbatim quotes from siblings (including ones from me and my typically developing brother) under various subtopics, which we have contextualized. At the end of those chapters, we have synthesized the various issues presented and provided practical suggestions for dealing with them.

Sibling Stories also includes three appendices. The first discusses things to consider when planning for the future of a person with ASD and is intended as a springboard for siblings wishing to be proactive about this often difficult issue. The second offers strategies for discussing ASD with family members and people in the community. The last appendix lists selected resources on ASD that typical siblings and others might find useful. This list will enable interested people to become more educated regarding ASD, among other things.

We hope *Sibling Stories* will serve as a learning tool for siblings who want to make sense of their own experiences. Additionally, it is our hope that the information presented here will help parents better meet the emotional needs of their typically developing children, who often feel overlooked amid autism's shadow. Finally, we would like professionals working with families touched by ASD to gain new understanding of what life is like for siblings as they grow.

Above all, we know that *Sibling Stories* will inspire hope and serve as a testament to the rich life journey experienced by brothers and sisters of people with ASD.

Lynne Stern Feiges and Mary Jane Weiss
Winter 2004

Chapter 1

The Sibling Connection: Explaining and Sharing the Experience of Being a Brother or Sister of a Person with ASD

It doesn't matter how much time has elapsed or how far we've traveled.
Our brothers and sisters bring us face to face with our former selves
and remind us how intricately bound up we are in each other's lives.
— Jane Mersky Leder (Brothers and Sisters, 1991)

The nature of the sibling bond is a complex one. The connection is often intense, and it is usually lifelong. Even under the best of circumstances, sibling relationships are often fraught with feelings of jealousy and competition. Yet, sibling connections also remain one of the greatest sources of solace in life. Siblings know us from before we knew anyone else and not only remember our histories (as good friends do), but also share our histories. This is the unique feature of the sibling connection, and what makes it essentially irreplaceable.

While the strength of sibling bonds can differ tremendously and be characterized by varying levels of negative and positive affect, sibling-hood is always a central point of definition for an individual. For instance, most young siblings define themselves at least in part as a brother or sister; and, even as adults, siblings continue to feel linked to this role. Having a strong sibling relationship has become increasingly more important in recent times, as life span extends, and as divorce and remarriage remain prevalent (Bank & Kahn, 1982). In contrast to other relationships that are vulnerable to loss through various types of life transitions, many times an enduring sense of refuge accompanies the sibling relationship, especially in adulthood.

In this chapter, we will explore sibling relationships in general and examine how they change over time. From there, we will talk about what researchers have learned regarding brothers and sisters of people with disabilities, particularly when that disability is an autism spectrum disorder (ASD). Finally, the siblings who told their stories for *Sibling Stories* will be introduced.

The Sibling Relationship

The process of adapting to siblinghood begins with the birth of a new baby. This is especially true if the new baby is the second child in the family, but the birth of every new child increases the need for reassur-ance and attention on the part of the older child or children. Parents can facilitate the adjustment process by talking to the sibling about the baby and by meeting that sibling's need for emotional support and attention (Cicirelli, 1995).

Older siblings tend to be leaders from the start and models for their younger brothers and sisters (Cicirelli, 1995). As the younger sib-ling gets older and more capable of reciprocal and imaginative play, older siblings often become more interested in the younger sibling (Dunn, 1992). Play is the context in which sibling relationships take form, the place where siblings learn to share, pretend, and simply have fun. "Our sisters and brothers play leading roles in the day to day reality of our childhood experience – as our competitors, true, but also as our peers, our first real partners in life" (Merrell, 1995, p. 12).

As many of us know, factors such as gender and closeness in age definitely impact upon the sibling connection. In general, siblings closer in age are likely to develop a closer emotional bond, although they are also likely to experience more arguments and difficulty in getting along (Buhrmester, 1992). Strong sibling bonds are most likely to occur when children are the same gender, are close in age, and have many shared activities and interests. Conversely, wider age discrepancies, varying genders, and separate activities result in weaker sibling bonding (Bank & Kahn, 1982).

It is typical for young sibling relationships to be characterized by a great deal of affection and caretaking. As siblings age, however, the relationship becomes more reciprocal. In other words, the older sibling does less nurturing, and both siblings interact more equally. This is especially likely to happen in middle childhood, or from ages 9 to 12, when siblings begin to share social activities such as sports or arts and crafts. As siblings age, they may develop common interests, such as horseback riding or skateboarding. However, even if their interests diverge, there is a capacity for siblings to share in one another's interests, to coach one another in honing a skill, or to admire one another's achievements (Dunn, 1992).

During early and middle childhood, there is usually substantial conflict between siblings. Early on, this may take the form of fighting over toys. This conflict continues about sharing objects, with each sibling strongly focused on identifying objects belonging to him- or herself. There are also conflicts around parental attention, fairness, and access to various privileges, among other things.

These types of sibling conflicts tend to diminish substantially by late adolescence (Buhrmester, 1992). At this time, most of us have lives and connections independent of the family, so family no longer plays the only or central role in support or companionship. It is not that the sibling or family relationships have lost importance; it is simply that the world of the adolescent has expanded and has integrated many new social players. While this expansion of the social world reduces a sibling's dependency on family members for social contact, it also reduces the stress on the sibling bond and enables the adolescent to experience powerful and important positive peer relationships outside the family context.

Finally, in adulthood, siblings remain an important point of contact for many adults, even though the nature of adult sibling relationships vary.

For example, there are often mutual struggles requiring a fair amount of cooperation and planning, such as managing parents' ailing health and coping with the loss of parents. Also, after parents die, sisters and brothers remain one of the few if only connections to each other's earliest stages of life, including deeply felt childhood memories and experiences.

When a Sibling Has a Disability

Because we do not choose our siblings, it is up to each of us to manage the advantages and disadvantages of the relationships we are born into (Merrell, 1995). Most of us find ways to celebrate the positive aspects and accept the disappointments, such as personality conflicts or major disagreements. However, this process is vastly more complex when one sibling has a disability.

In early childhood, the awareness of the sibling's disabling condition is often minimal (Lobato, 1983, 1990). Nevertheless, siblings tend to express concern over a brother or sister's disability. They see their parents' stress and distress, experience disruption in family life and activities due to the threat or occurrence of challenging behaviors, and often perceive an inequity in the division of attention between children (Lobato, 1983, 1990; Lobato, Faust, & Spirato, 1988). There may also be a perception or demand on the parents' part that a sibling should completely accept the family member's disability – even where the sibling is not yet developmentally able to do so (Gamble & Woulbroun, 1993).

Once there is a solid awareness, the issue of adaptation arises. How a typical sibling adapts to a brother or sister's disability is influenced by a number of factors. Sisters tend to experience more negative effects of the stress of having a sibling with a disability and are likely to take on a caretaking role (McHale & Gamble, 1987, 1989). Brothers, on the other hand, tend to have more outside, peer-based interests and activities that insulate them from some of the disability's impact. (Therefore, it is important for parents to monitor the levels of caretaking by daughters and to nurture outside interests and peer relationships for typically developing siblings of both genders.) Additionally, older children tend to fare better, probably due to their increased capacities for perspective taking and understanding the complexities of personalities and the impact of a disability. For example, an older child can comprehend that her brother is not talking because he is not able to, while a younger sibling may wonder whether his sister is just being difficult.

Adjustment also appears to be better in larger families. That is, if the typical sibling has at least one other typical sibling, adjustment is often better. This is likely due to the possibility of shared caretaking and the provision of mutual emotional support (Dyson, 1989; Lobato, 1990).

The data on birth order and age difference are variable. Some reports suggest that older sisters and younger brothers have more struggles in adjustment, but findings are not always consistent. It does seem clear, however, that closeness in age between the typical sibling and the sibling with a disability is associated with increased adjustment difficulties for the typical sibling (Cicirelli, 1995). This is not surprising, given that siblings close in age have similar interests, similar needs for attention, and high levels of competition and jealousy. When there is a larger age span, the typical sibling generally has more access to individual attention from parents and, therefore, does not feel the sibling competition so keenly.

Not surprisingly, one of the most influential factors in a sibling's adjustment is the functioning level of the brother or sister with a disability. That is, the higher the functioning level of the child with the disability, the better the adjustment of the typical child (Cicirelli, 1995). Also, when the sibling with a disability engages in behavior that is embarrassing or has an appearance or behaviors that are bizarre, adjustment problems for the typical sibling are common (Boyce & Barnett, 1993). Of course, children are raised by parents and are affected by their parents' emotional health and ability to provide a nurturing emotional environment. Siblings are, therefore, significantly influenced by how well their parents are coping with the stress of parenting a child with a disability. If parents have difficulty communicating or suffer from depression, for example, the typical sibling's adjustment might be poor (Dyson, Edgar, & Crnic, 1989; McHale, Sloan, & Simeonsson, 1986).

One of the ways in which having a sibling with a disability alters the normal course of events is that typical developmental processes and transitions may not occur. For example, research has shown that roles are not normative in families with a child with retardation. This means that typical siblings assume a dominant role, regardless of their own age relative to the sibling with retardation (Brody, Stoneman, Davis, & Crapps, 1991; Stoneman, Brody, Davis, & Crapps, 1987, 1988). In addition, adolescence does not transform the sibling relationship when one sibling has a disability as it does when both siblings are typical. That is, typical siblings continue to have a dominant relationship with their sibling with a disability, instead of developing the more egalitarian relationships common among typical siblings as they grow older (Cicirelli, 1995). In some cases, this hinders the typical adolescent in developing more egalitarian relationships in general. For example, a typical sibling may try to dominate conversations or be aggressive about decision making with friends.

Adolescence poses many other difficulties as well. For example, if caretaking responsibilities are extensive, the typical teen will be hampered in developing an independent and active social life outside of the home. In addition, the sense of stigma attached to having a sibling with a disability may be prominent at this stage of life, where peer acceptance and fitting in are so crucial. This can serve to further heighten feelings of isolation and fears of rejection (Cicirelli, 1995).

Reasons for Optimism

A discussion of the effects of having a sibling with a disability would be incomplete without addressing the potential positive impact of this experience. Research in adolescents with and without siblings with disabilities has shown that levels of self-efficacy – belief in oneself to accomplish goals – are equivalent in these groups (O'Kane, Grissom, & Borkowski, 2002). Thus, as might otherwise be expected, adolescents who have a sibling with a disability are not behind their peers in this important set of beliefs. Additional data from the same study point to the importance of maternal modeling of prosocial and empathic behavior. Hence, the positive adaptation of the mother clearly influences the self-efficacy of the typical sibling, highlighting the link between parental coping and sibling adjustment. Not surprisingly, therefore, in our interviews, several siblings highlighted their admiration for their mothers, whom they viewed as models of understanding and strength. Exposure to good role models for adapting to unexpected circumstances bodes well for the development of positive self-concept and good coping skills.

Another positive finding is that lower levels of conflict are reported between typical siblings and those with disabilities, compared to interactions between typical siblings in other families. While it is possible that this may be the result of parental pressure for siblings to get along, it is also possible that the relationship between the former set of siblings naturally engenders low levels of tension. Along the same lines, other researchers have found that siblings of children with Down's Syndrome showed markedly higher levels of affection and nurturing than siblings of typical children (Abramovich, Stanhope, Pepler, & Corter, 1987).

One of the early studies in this area sheds some light on the inconsistencies in the effects of having a brother or sister with a disability on typical siblings. Grossman (1972) found that adolescent siblings who had grown up with a sibling with retardation expressed a great deal of variability in their responses regarding the effects of the experience. While some emphasized resentment toward their parents or sibling, restrictions on their social life, embarrassment and shame regarding the sibling with a disability, and guilt over their own "typical" status, others emphasized the positive impact of the experience. That is, they often saw themselves as more mature, more compassionate, more tolerant, and more responsible than they might have been without this experience.

Other researchers have noted the same variable pattern. For example, McHale et al. (1986) found that siblings ages 6 to 15 largely said positive things about their brothers and sisters, regardless of whether their sibling was typically developing or had mental retardation or autism. However, some children did say negative things. Themes centered on worry over the future and feelings of unfair treatment by parents. As mentioned earlier, children reported more positive responses when they perceived their parents as responding positively to the situation. They were also helped by a good factual understanding of the disability. Thus, an understanding of the disability is critically important, as it protects the typical sibling from unwarranted fears and worries (Glasberg, 2000; Harris, 1994).

As with any other experience, each family has its own unique ways of dealing with having a member with a disability. Some families are ultimately strengthened by adversity, while others fall to its power. Several patterns have been found to be common in families with a child with a developmental disability (Siegel & Silverstein, 1994). Patterns of risk include the parentified child, the withdrawn child, the acting-out child, and the super-achieving child. Siegel and Silverstein make a strong argument that the family's acceptance of the disability affords siblings the greatest protections against these patterns. Families who communicate well, who make time for each child, who solve problems effectively, and who access support are in the best position to assist the typical sibling in adjusting to life in a family with a member who has a disability.

In brief, while some studies have pointed to the existence of more adjustment problems in children of siblings with disabilities (e.g., Gold, 1993), others have reported no major negative impact or effects (e.g., McHale et al., 1986). So, generally, there does not appear to be a relationship between having a sibling with a disability and increased problems in adjustment (Lobato et al., 1988).

When the Disability Is an Autism Spectrum Disorder

In general, most children growing up with a sibling with ASD do not show any major negative effects from the experience (Grissom & Borkowski, 2002; McHale et al., 1986). Nevertheless, parents of children with ASD have reported more concerns about their typically developing children in both internalizing (e.g., depression, anxiety) and externalizing (e.g., aggression, defiance) problems, compared to parental reports on siblings of children with Down's Syndrome or without disabilities (Rodrigue, Geffken, & Morgan, 1993). However, while the frequency of these problems was higher in the group of children who had siblings with ASD, their levels of the behaviors were still in the normal range. Furthermore, their self-esteem was comparable to that of the other groups.

However, it cannot be denied that ASD poses some unique challenges to the sibling relationship. For example, having a brother or sister with ASD is perhaps more difficult than having a sibling with a different disability. Behavior problems in ASD are common, which may lead to both embarrassment and a curtailment of family activities. In addition, it may be harder to establish an emotionally close bond with a sibling with ASD, compared to a sibling with a different disability. This is because individuals with ASD usually have difficulty with the reciprocity of relationships, and with tasks such as perspective taking or empathizing. Kaminsky and Dewey (2001) found that siblings of children with ASD reported less nurturance, less sibling intimacy, and less positive interaction than siblings of individuals with Down's Syndrome or without disabilities. (Like many other researchers, however, these authors also noted some positive effects. For example, siblings of people with ASD reported great admiration for their brother or sister with ASD, and reported little competition.)

Another potential area of difficulty for siblings of people with ASD is the advent of early intervention services. As diagnosis has improved, children with ASD are receiving services at younger and younger ages. Much of this intervention – including intensive applied behavior analysis (ABA) programs – takes place in the home, which means that siblings are exposed to a great deal of specialized treatment there. In an intensive ABA program, for example, instructors might be working on helping the child with ASD ask for things she wants, imitate actions, identify common objects, play appropriately with toys, or answer questions. Instructors might also be working on increasing the child's willingness to learn or reducing behaviors that interfere with learning.

The child with ASD may earn access to special treats or activities when involved in this instruction and, as a result, there can be jealousy about the levels of attention the child receives and/or special privileges. Additionally, siblings may resent the extent to which the therapy schedule affects family life and the substantial amount of time and resources parents devote to working with their child with ASD or organizing the home instruction.

As shown, parental communication is a key variable in helping typical siblings adapt to their family life. Without clear communication, children tend to create their own explanations for things that are confusing or difficult to comprehend (Lobato, 1993). They may create mythical explanations for the disability in general, for behaviors exhibited by a sibling, or for a particular treatment mode, such as time-out. Some of these explanations may incorrectly lay blame on parents or on the typical siblings themselves. Providing typical siblings with clear and accurate information at a developmentally appropriate level, therefore, goes a long way toward increasing their adjustment (Glasberg, 2000; McHale et al., 1986; Simeonsson & McHale, 1981).

Surprisingly, typically developing siblings seem to understand less than we might expect. For example, Glasberg (2000) found that while siblings understood more about ASD with age, their understanding developed at a somewhat delayed rate compared to understandings of other illnesses. She also found that parents of children with autism overestimated their typical children's understanding of the disorder. It may be that ASD is a particularly difficult concept to grasp, given the deficits and variability associated with it. It also may be that there is a genuine gap between what Brodzinsky has called "telling vs. understanding": While parents tell their typically developing children a great deal about ASD, their children may fail to truly comprehend its nature and impact (Brodzinsky, Pappas, Singer, & Braff, 1981; Brodzinsky, Schechter, & Brodzinsky, 1986). Parents should therefore probe whether their typically developing children have grasped the vocabulary and concepts covered in the discussions of the disability. It is vital for parents to frequently revisit the topic, to match what is told to the child's developmental level, and to assess whether the child understands what has been shared.

The Siblings Who Shared Their Experiences with Us

The available research shows us that siblings of people with ASD share certain commonalities. However, we also know that the path of every sibling is unique. In light of this, the interviewees we chose for inclusion in this book were selected, in part, because of their differences. The 20 siblings featured here are diverse in a number of respects, including their ages, family composition, and level of involvement with their brother or sister with ASD. The severity of the disability also varied from family to family. Some families faced a profound level of autism requiring residential treatment, while others presented more high-functioning or even "curable" difficulties. In any event, the reader will see that these siblings' stories are as singular as ASD itself.

Anna Reed: Anna, a 38-year-old social worker living outside a major city, is the youngest in her family, in which there are four siblings. Her brother Joseph has autism and is 42 years old. He lives with their parents, who have been married a long time. Joseph has a range of strengths, including reading Shakespeare, graduating from high school on time, obtaining a degree at a community college, and holding a job at a pharmacy for 20 years.

Jeremy Plant: Jeremy is an 18-year-old from Wisconsin. His parents divorced when he was in the 5th grade, and he now lives with his father and his new wife. Eli, who is 6 years younger than Jeremy, has mild autism and lives in a group home several nights per week. The rest of the time he spends with Jeremy and his father. Eli is in a general education classroom and does fairly well in school. He also has a great sense of what is right or wrong. He'll tell everyone, for instance, that they need to wear their seatbelts!

Olivia Hanover: Forty-year-old Olivia is a special education teacher and the eldest of five children. Her brother Matthew, who is 13 years younger than her, has profound autism and lives at a group home. Additionally, her son, Joshua, has mild autism. Olivia lives in a town in New Jersey where there are at least 32 documented cases of autism in children. She would like to find out where the link is, especially whether it is environmentally based.

Becky Lott: Becky is 32 years old and lives in Virginia. She is the eldest of three siblings, including her 28-year-old brother, Gordon, who has autism. Gordon has always lived at home with their parents and attended special education classes. He holds a job and does various activities around the house, like cutting the lawn and bringing in the groceries. Becky says he has always been very self-sufficient.

Julie Shore: Julie is a self-assured 12-year-old who lives at home with her parents and her brother, Robby, who is 10 years old and has autism. Robby attends a special education classroom in a public elementary school. Julie is glad her brother has learned to read because, she says, it has brought him back into her and her parents' world a bit. Her mom is president of their local autism society chapter, and sometimes Julie goes to meetings with her.

Jessica Golden: There are three siblings in Jessica's family. A special education teacher, she is 30 and the eldest. Her middle brother, Will, was diagnosed with autism when he was 3 or 4 years old. When her parents divorced several years later, the children subsequently lived with their mother. After receiving services at a private placement, Will made strides in language and cognition, which was deemed a "recovery." His diagnosis then changed to "gifted and talented/learning disabled." He was mainstreamed completely, and later attended college and graduate school. He holds a government job and plans to marry.

Sarah Cooper: Sarah, 31, grew up in New Jersey. Her brother, Rick, is 15 months younger than her and was diagnosed when he was about 3. Rick, who also has tuberous sclerosis — a congenital genetic disease characterized by tuber-like growths on the brain and other organs — was placed at a private school soon after his diagnosis and moved to the program's group home a few years later. Sarah and Rick's parents separated when Sarah was 7. Sarah says that her brother's tuberous sclerosis has always been more threatening to her than the autism, which she says was kind of secondhand.

Ashley Williams: Teenaged Ashley is three years older than her brother, Todd. She was 6 when her brother received a diagnosis of autism, which, she says, she accepts as something that has always been a part of her life. Todd attends a day program and lives at home with Ashley and their parents. Ashley sometimes participates in a sibling support group that is a branch of the support group her parents attend.

Dana and Susan Peters: Dana, 25, and Susan, 22, have a 21-year-old brother with autism, Chris. Chris, who is considered average on the autism spectrum, was diagnosed when he was about 3 or 4, and started a private program soon after. The family lived together at home and had assistance from a nanny, who played a very influential role in Chris' development. According to Dana and Susan, Chris' condition has always been very accepted both in their immediate and extended family.

Bethany Powers: Bethany, 36, is a writer living in New England. She is the youngest of three female children. Her sister Emma, 40, was diagnosed with autism when she was an adult. Before that, she was labeled emotionally disturbed and also schizophrenic. Emma is extraordinarily bright and flexible for someone with autism, says Bethany. She has lived unsupervised in her own apartment for many years and holds a job at a candy company. Bethany adds that she, much more than her parents, is the family member who is most connected to Emma. Bethany wrote her first novel about a boy with autism and his twin sister. In fact, she wrote the first chapter of the book after handling a crisis with Emma.

Lynne Stern Feiges and Michael Stern: Lynne, 38, and Michael, 39, are the first and second children in a family with four siblings. Their brother Rich, 36, spent more than 25 years at a private program and lived in a group home starting in early adolescence. He has accomplished much in his life, including learning to read and write, but aggressive behavior necessitated that he leave his group home placement in favor of a more restrictive program. Seth, the youngest child of the family, also has developmental impairments. Their parents have been together for 40 years and counting.

Sam, Jamie, Leslie, and Jordan Cohen: There are five children in the Cohen family: Sam, 54; Jamie, 53; Leslie, 50; Jordan, 48; and Marc, 45, who has autism. The family grew up in Kansas and lost their dad when they were young. Their mother, a strong figure, lived to see and celebrate Marc settling into his own apartment. The siblings are now scattered across the country, but all maintain strong ties with Marc.

Richard Flynn: Just 9 years old, Richard is a happy 4th grader with a good disposition. He is able to talk articulately about his 4-year-old brother, David, who has autism. The two share a bunk bed, and Richard often gets David his breakfast without even being asked. According to the boys' mother, David stopped talking when he was 2 and became unhappy around the same time. He was eventually diagnosed at age 3.

Maryann Hall: Maryann is 12 years old and lives in the Midwest. Her 16-year-old sister, Christine, has Down's Syndrome and autism. The family lives together at home and receives respite care from time to time. Christine is in a special education class at the public high school. Their mother suspects a genetic component to Christine's disabilities, pointing out that there are several children with autism on her husband's side of the family.

Lance Strong: Lance is an athletic 13-year-old who lives in Virginia. His younger brother, Michael, who is now 10, was 3 years old when he was diagnosed with autism. Lance says that his brother's memory is incredible and that he reads and writes. He also acknowledges that he knows Michael's autism has not been easy for his parents.

Authors' Note
We have changed the names and some of the identifying details of the interviewees, with the exception of Lynne Stern Feiges and her brothers. All of the quotes attributed to interviewees appear verbatim to ensure the accuracy and completeness of their views and feelings. The highlighted quotes appearing in Chapter 6 were written by the authors and represent a composite of statements expressed to us by different people during our research for this book.

Chapter 2

The Family Impact: Understanding and Integrating ASD into Family Life

B eing part of a family with a member with ASD can cause typical siblings to feel separate from people they perceive as having a more idealized family life. That is because families that must integrate ASD into their lives face certain circumstances and complexities that remain foreign to families without a member with a disability. For instance, the presence of ASD exerts pressure on family communication, marriage, and relationships with friends. And typical siblings, in particular, can be highly affected by their parents' search for a diagnosis, choice of treatments, and handling of difficult or disruptive behaviors exhibited by the child with ASD.

We asked siblings how they thought their families were impacted by the demands posed by ASD. Listen as they describe how they and their families dealt with these various demands, and also what the general atmosphere was like at home.

Learning About ASD

In every family we met and interviewed for this book, there is a story of how and when the family started perceiving a problem. In some cases, it is a prolonged period of worry followed by a confirming diagnosis. In other families, there is an unspoken fear and a reluctance to speak openly about any worries over the development of a family member. In a few families, there is total acceptance. In all cases, siblings perceive both the problem and the family's preferred manner of dealing with it.

In the stories that follow, we can sense each sibling's desire for understanding, each sibling's fears and worries, and the hope siblings had that their fears would be unfounded. We also sense their knowledge that indeed something was awry in their brother or sister's development.

Something Was "Different"

Anna Reed: My mother always knew something was different with Joseph. He started language development and then stopped. They would take him for testing because he was physically slow to develop as well. The story was that when my next brother was born and my mom went away for three days, Joseph was traumatized and fell to his knees crying. He thought she was never coming back. He stopped talking and then developed speech again.

Julie Shore: I knew he was weird. He was always going to the hospital, always getting tests. He used to be very verbal and then he lost it [language] at 18 months.

Sarah Cooper: I was pretty much oblivious to Rick's autism growing up. I knew he was different from me in terms of language and behavior. Rick was like a monkey, really. He was not a normal child. He would jump off refrigerators, he would climb up people, jump out of his two-story bedroom window. He would tear the guts out of a television, try to climb in. He would get out of his harness in bed. But it felt normal to me. I didn't think anything was wrong, but I knew Rick was different and I was in a different situation. But I never thought of it as something being wrong or off-kilter. I don't recall it ever being explained to me, but they didn't try and shelter me from it.

Jordan Cohen: I remember my parents taking him to the University of Kansas Medical Center when he was 3 or 4 for different diagnostic tests. We noticed something wrong when he didn't speak. I was driving in a car with my parents, and I remember telling them that Marc didn't talk so he probably wouldn't go to school. He [in fact] didn't go to school. The school district said they didn't have anything for him. All of us knew that something was wrong. They began to tell us that he was different. I must have been 6 or 7, and I remember taking Marc aside and saying, "Marc, you've got to act normal now. You've got to come out of whatever this is. It's time."

Leslie Cohen: It was apparent at a young age that he was different. There was a five-year age difference between us, so when he was 3 or 4, I noticed he wasn't as verbal, and his motor skills. In terms of the autism itself, that wasn't a term that was thrown around very much in the early 60s. We became more aware of it after he was institutionalized and diagnosed. Jamie and I started reading about it. We investigated it on our own.

Dana Peters: Everything was pretty normal with Chris. Then he just stopped developing or interacting with other kids and became hyperactive. Everyone kind of blew this off. I didn't realize anything was wrong; I was not conscious of all of it, but I knew he wasn't talking.

Becky Lott: We knew he didn't talk, so my parents took him to children's hospital. All these doctors said he was retarded. He was a slow learner. This didn't bother me.

Jessica Golden: In 1973-74, he stopped talking. He was very social when he was 18 months – even more outgoing than me! They didn't know if he was deaf or not listening.

Jeremy Plant: When he was young, he wouldn't respond to things right away. He was slower with his talking and developing in general.

The Diagnosis

Perhaps the most heart-wrenching stories are those of families trying to get answers and searching for diagnoses. When families "know" something is wrong, they desperately need expertise in labeling the problem, explaining its origins, and choosing interventions. Even with society's increased awareness of ASD and the publicity surrounding it, some families spend years searching fruitlessly for answers. Along the way, siblings sometimes misunderstand how and why their brother or sister acts so peculiarly. The stories below provide a glimpse of the agonizing and often confusing journeys of so many families.

Anna Reed: Over the years, they got different diagnoses. My mother would get one (e.g., retardation or schizophrenia) and just knew it was wrong. So, she'd give up. They'd get upset and then stop pursuing the issue. But I guess the right information was hard to find.

Olivia Hanover: Matthew's pediatrician didn't really pick up on anything, but my mother knew because he was the youngest of five and didn't make eye contact. He didn't really cry with tears. Then he ultimately didn't have proper language skills and was referred to a specialist in New York, who diagnosed autism. He was 4 or 5 years old; shortly after that, he was sent to [a school in central New Jersey].

Jessica Golden: When he was diagnosed, the reports blamed my mother for being a young mom. She was in her mid-20s!

Jordan Cohen: When he was 5, 6, 7, we began to hear the term "autism" from the professionals. At the time, Bettelheim was influential … refrigerator parents, etc. I think the presumption was, in my mom's case, because she worked and my grandmother did the childcare, that perhaps that accounted for the autism.

Leslie Cohen: When I was 5, I was babysitting Marc and he fell out of the crib and broke his collarbone. For years I thought that was why he was autistic, because he fell out of the crib. I thought, Oh god, it's all my fault that he fell out of the crib.

Second Generation of Symptoms

Olivia Hanover: When my son Joshua was diagnosed, my husband handled it great – better than I did. The issue of having a special needs child, I didn't dwell on that because we had tried so long to have a child. When I went for tests during my pregnancy, I would analyze the tests until my ob/gyn told me to "just chill out." He was born, had Apgars of 9 and 10. Up until his first year, he was a very happy child. He walked early, loved people. If anything, he was the complete opposite of what my brother was. But on the spectrum of the rainbow, my brother is very profound, whereas my son is not. I kept saying to my pediatrician that something was wrong. I knew there was something there because he started to isolate himself. He didn't do the spinning or have a lot of the stims that the typical autistic child has. But something wasn't right, and so I took him to a neurologist. When I went, I was very hesitant to bring up my brother because I knew immediately they were going to pigeon hole Joshua into an autism category – and I wanted to make sure that he truly was. I think too many kids are misdiagnosed to their detriment.

Family Communication

Once a diagnosis has been made, one of the central tasks confronting parents of a child with ASD is communicating to the rest of the family about the disability (see suggestions in Appendix B). Every family does it differently, and each parent finds a way that feels comfortable to him or her. The presentation must match the developmental levels of the typical siblings. Thus, while a very young child may need the simplest explanation and a little reassurance, an older child may be eager to learn about the disorder in more detail and what the future will bring.

The explanation given lays a foundation for how the siblings will cope with this reality throughout their lifetimes. For example, how ASD is explained and discussed affects how siblings perceive and interact with their brother or sister with ASD. It will also influence how effectively they can collaborate with their parents in ensuring that the family functions to the benefit of all its members. In addition, the nature and tone of the explanation affect how siblings will explain the behaviors and characteristics of ASD to their friends.

A good explanation may make siblings feel less fearful of ASD itself and of their brother or sister. A poor explanation, on the other hand, may fuel anxiety, and impede the development of a reciprocal relationship with the sibling with ASD. It may also create guilt feelings of how ASD entered the family, fears of personally developing ASD, or embarrassment over the existence of ASD in the family.

A parent explaining ASD to a sibling may be emotionally overwrought with his or her own reactions to the news of a child's diagnosis. As you can hear in the excerpts below, however, siblings have their individual emotional reactions — which may even be discrepant from those of their other typical siblings. While many shared their feelings with parents and other family members, others experienced some feelings of isolation.

Explaining ASD Within the Family

Jeremy Plant: I remember my parents coming home, and I overheard them saying the umbilical cord was wrapped around his neck. I'm pretty sure that was part of the cause. It was explained to me when I was a little older that he (a) is just not normal, (b) will be normal in some things (and it will be more difficult in other areas for him to learn), and (c) has a 5 percent chance of outgrowing it and becoming a fully functional person. I was devastated by this news. I was hoping for a brother whom I could teach to play baseball, basketball, and football. To pretty much have a little brother, because I was always complaining when I was about 5 or 6 that I didn't have a brother.

Julie Shore: I can remember my parents explaining how he was going to be different. That he wasn't going to talk as much. I don't remember my parents telling me about autism, but I don't think I was asking 'cause I could tell something was wrong.

Maryann Hall: I noticed she was acting kind of strange, so I asked my parents. They told me that she's different from others and that she has Down's Syndrome and autism. I didn't know what it was, so I asked how she got that way. They said it was kind of hard to explain and didn't really explain it to me. They just said some kids get that and some don't. I really didn't understand it after that. I thought it was just like people who can't walk and have to be in a wheelchair. Just like that.

Dana Peters: What I remember, in terms of an explanation from my parents, was that "Your brother is different, and we all have to help him." I look back, and think I accepted it pretty easily. Now, because he is an adult, we talk about it more.

Susan Peters: I don't remember one particular lecture. I was just figuring it out for myself, and my parents explained that he was different and what that meant for us. I knew that it meant it would be harder for him and that as his older sister, I had more responsibility growing up.

Michael Stern: I learned about autism at a young age, maybe 11 or 12. At the time, Rich had been misdiagnosed for years. We had never heard the term autism mentioned until that time. I was told that nobody really knows its causes. It was explained as a mental condition that causes a person to withdraw into their own little eggshell. My parents did not share a lot of their trials and tribulations with me. They have a tendency to internalize a lot of their problems in an attempt to shield their children.

Jamie Cohen: We learned about Marc's condition from our parents, who didn't have very much information at all. They said it was a communications disorder and that he lives in his own private world. I remember that some of the doctors said stuff that I just consider really stupid, like "He behaves bizarrely."

Anna Reed: It's so obvious to others that he is disabled, and yet it's part of the family secret in not acknowledging it. The anxiety in this family is different than some other families I have seen. You even take a family that's low income, where the expectation for their child is different. They just accept this child as really disabled and it's sort of like, "Oh well. This is really a hard life but let's see what we can do with it." Rather than, "Oh my god, he's not meeting this huge expectation that we have for all our children and isn't this horrible ... Isn't life horrible! A terrible crisis that he's like this, and if we work hard enough and do it right, maybe he can become more." Everything is important and upsetting.

In It Together: Parents and Typical Siblings

Jamie Cohen: My mom shared a lot with us because she was always concerned about him. She treated us all like partners and made us all concerned with his welfare.

Lance Strong: I feel free to talk about it with my parents, if I notice something. They know it's hard on me and on them. It's something we all know. I kind of accept it. I view his autism as an external thing. Something that's covering him up ... that everything is normal inside but the autism is holding him back.

My parents talk about possible things they could do for Michael and what some of the problems are. They talk to each other, but it's at the dinner table, so I'm present. There's nothing emotionally scarring or traumatic about hearing it. Nothing I wish I was protected from. And, I kinda like to know it, too.

I know it hasn't been easy for them. My dad said one time that Michael was the hardest thing he's ever had in his life. I was mildly surprised by this.

Ashley Williams: Since I was only 6 when my brother was diagnosed, I was never really a part of trying to find out about autism or treatment for him. Yet, as I have become older, my parents have – or at least I felt they have – shared everything with me about trying to help Todd. I don't think I could have been more protected even if I wanted to be. I always would have been conscious of what was going on with Todd.

Becky Lott: My parents were understanding about me having a hard time about Gordon – because they were too! They had never dealt with anything like this before, and they didn't know how to deal with Gordon either in the beginning. Now we can just take him with a grain of salt. He has a bad day, we understand, and we know he'll get over it

Disconnection by Eldest Sibling

Dana Peters: Because I was 4 years older than Chris, I think growing up I was kind of exempt in a way. I don't feel guilty, because I feel like I will have my chance to step up to the plate.

Sam Cohen: My parents didn't share anything that I recall. I felt like I was kind of disconnected from everyone else in the family. I was the oldest and developing more of a life on my own than anyone else was. If he weren't in my life, it wouldn't be much different. My siblings' lives would be, but mine wouldn't.

Michael Stern: I never really had the desire to understand autism. I guess this was a subconscious byproduct of my desire to ignore my brother's problem and to negate his existence.

Explaining ASD to Peers

Typical siblings all face the issue of explaining ASD to others. It is a disability that is not easily ignored, and the behaviors and characteristics of individuals with ASD merit some discussion in most contexts. Especially during adolescence, siblings struggle with if and how to explain ASD to others. Many try to avoid discussing the problems of their brother or sister. Inevitably, however, explanations are required. (See Appendix B for suggestions about how to discuss ASD.) Many siblings end up defining ASD in inaccurate and somewhat inarticulate ways. This usually reflects the lack of specific information they personally possess about ASD. In some ways, ASD is an enigma to many typical siblings. Nevertheless, the knowledge that they do have centers on the unusual and bizarre behaviors they see their siblings demonstrate. Fears of rejection and of embarrassment permeate the excerpts below.

How Siblings Explain

Dana Peters: To friends, I'd tell them that he is different. But I was out of the house more than I had people over. This was more comfortable and easier for my parents.

Sam Cohen: I explained autism as best I could, but it really didn't come up. He wasn't around because he went to the state school. It was accepted that he wasn't around, more or less.

Julie Shore: I usually tell my friends that my brother's autistic; he's a little bit like retarded. He's smart but acts retarded.

Jeremy Plant: When I explain his condition to others, I say, "Well, my brother's autistic, and they say, 'What's that?' It's a disability not like retarded but it's not perfect and normal, it's somewhere in between. Sometimes he can get loud and he might ask you some real stupid questions and stuff like that. Don't be offended."

Ashley Williams: I don't remember ever sitting down with my mom or dad and discussing autism. But it seems like I've always known what autism was. Whenever I explain autism to my friends, I rattle off the literal definition: "Autism is a developmental disability that occurs in 10-15 out of every 10,000 births, four times as more likely to occur in boys than girls." Then I begin to tell them about Todd and my personal experiences. I tell them how he'll never be cured, that he is supposedly functioning at the level of a 2-year-old, and that he has little verbal skill except when he wants something. Then I tell them that he has a great personality, is always smiling, and that I love him to death. I never avoid the topic of autism with my friends.

Jordan Cohen: My friends were interested and asked me to explain autism. I said, "Marc lives in his own world." That's about as articulate as I was then.
Jamie Cohen: When I was a little kid, I didn't explain Marc. I didn't know how. I didn't talk about it. Eventually I would talk about it as I got older, but I was always afraid people wouldn't accept it.

Lynne Stern Feiges: I was relieved when the movie *Rain Man* came out. For so long, it was hard to explain to people what exactly autism was. Hard to verbalize all that. The best I could do was tell people it was "like retarded." So, when the movie depicted all the sibling conflict and the compulsive attributes of Dustin Hoffman's autistic character, it was like a validation of what I'd been seeing and feeling for years. I told everyone I knew to see it and dragged my boyfriend to the movie. I even went to the stage door of a Broadway play starring Dustin Hoffman, and when he came outside, I called out to him that I was glad he won the Oscar for the movie. I wanted to thank him for it!

Olivia Hanover: I was in high school at the beginning of his treatment. No one really could explain what autism was – this was way before *Rain Man* or anything. Now people are more educated. I can remember pushing him in a stroller in a store – the "curse" that these [autistic] people have is that they're absolutely beautiful – and people wanted to talk to him. I'd explain that he was autistic and they'd look at me like I was crazy. They'd say what's that, and I'd say I can't really tell you, he's just autistic.

Fear of Rejection

Jordan Cohen: I was afraid to bring kids home, afraid they wouldn't understand. I was selective in what I told people.

Michael Stern: Rich was always a sore subject for me to discuss with friends. I was ashamed of him, in particular his behavior in public. I did my best to hide my association with Rich. I would avoid family outings with him. A simple trip to the store made me very anxious that I was going to run into someone from school or the neighborhood. I consciously separated myself from Rich and the rest of my family because of my shame. I was afraid of kids making fun of me, which is ruinous to some preadolescents.

Avoidance

Lance Strong: I don't bring the autism up with friends. If they ask, I'll gladly tell them. I don't really like to talk about it. They seem to understand [my attitude], though they're curious.
Maryann Hall: My friends know what autism is because we read a book in class about it. They don't really ask me.

Susan Peters: When I was growing up, I didn't hide his autism, but I wasn't as vocal about it. All my friends knew, but I didn't talk about it.

Michael Stern: I didn't really explain it to my friends at all. They didn't really ask. Rich was just a strange, likeable kid to them.

What Others Think

Anna Reed: In college, I remember a friend telling me [Joseph] was disabled, and it still came as a shock to me that he could see it that clearly. It made me relieved and also sad. Part of me wants his disability to go away, and if he's disabled, it doesn't go away and there's no chance for changing. Part of me does wish we could fix it.

Sarah Cooper: I would tell people that my brother was autistic and they'd look at me and say, "Autistic? Does he paint?" They'd always confuse that. People would correct me and think I was trying to say "artistic." It's really condescending.

My mom was very public about it. I didn't have to tell anyone on the block that my brother was autistic because everyone knew about it. There were a lot of newspaper articles, television news. Rick was this star of the community. I was lucky I didn't have to do a lot of explaining when I was young.

Treating ASD

A great deal of family energy goes into securing treatment for the child with ASD. In the past, institutionalizing individuals with ASD was more commonplace. This wracked many families with sorrow and guilt, but also provided the only viable treatment option and means to protect the well-being of other family members. The grim realities of institutional life included loss of freedom, inadequate mental health treatment, and poor custodial care. For example, it was possible for a person with ASD to spend an entire day rocking or being tied to a bed. The luckier families had the option of community-based group homes, which provided a family-like setting and a better opportunity for growth/learning. While these were generally more humane alternatives, they still separated the siblings in a permanent and undeniable way.

Every typical sibling has memories and stories to share regarding the search for treatment, the unusual aspects of treatments tried, and the impact that such treatments had upon them individually and as a family.

The Search for Treatment

Dana Peters: I have vivid memories of taking him to speech therapy. When that didn't work out, we took him to Montessori school, to another special ed program. I didn't think there was this impending doom, but I was confused. I was somewhat removed then, and in retrospect, I'm definitely more emotional about it now. I don't know if I was blocking it out at the time. I was along for the ride ... and I knew my brother was different. For so long, they said nothing was wrong with Chris. "He's a boy, he's just delayed ..." In the beginning, the most important thing was just finding a school for him. We were pretty much kept out of that. I don't remember discussing any of that, and I'm glad for this. It didn't confuse us and allowed us to just be kids – be ourselves.

Lynne Stern Feiges: I remember the search for treatment. We went from place to place on weekends, visiting different professionals and schools. There was the B vitamin doctor, the dilapidated school in this horrendous location by the airport, and, eventually, the program in Princeton where he ended up. I don't remember that they ever discussed what was going on more than just telling me where we were going. The tension in the car was unbelievable, though. I recall that one of them always went in and one of them stayed with us. What a balancing act. I can really appreciate this now.

Anna Reed: As far as being dragged all over while Joseph got help and special services, I wanted that because I don't think they did enough of it. I wanted them to take him to counseling! At least this would have acknowledged that we had a problem. They normalized it like there was no problem – and I knew it wasn't OK that he was this angry.

Jordan Cohen: My siblings and I would go to the library and read about autism. We would call doctors and explain Marc to whoever would answer the phone. The assumption was that we just had to find the right specialist ... the right treatment. I just remember my sisters dialing and dialing and dialing.

Jamie Cohen: I don't wish I was protected from it all. I just wanted him to be more protected! I wanted to force the doctors to understand more about him, give us some more answers.

Michael Stern: I recall the early years of going to a lot of doctors while my parents were trying to get Rich diagnosed. I understood that they were having difficulties finding the right diagnosis. I can't say that I empathized with their pain, only because I didn't have a full appreciation of it.

Institutionalization

Jordan Cohen: In 1966, Marc went to a state institution. My dad died, and a couple of months later, Marc was gone. It was very strange. A complete change in the way the family functioned. In another sense, it was a feeling of liberation, of being able to have the rest of us function as a normal family, go out, etc. I view the turning point of my life as my dad dying more than anything to do with Marc.

We looked at the state institution as custodial care. It was 150 miles away, and we'd visit him once a month. The concept of education was not thought of. It was warehousing people in cottages with locked doors. I remember coming down once and he had had an ashtray thrown at him. He still has the scars. A guiding thing for me has been the recognition that there are certain people viewed as expendable in society. A child with that type of cognitive disability was viewed as expendable – not worthy of education, or a minimal one at best.

Jamie Cohen: When my dad died, a great-aunt of ours recommended he be institutionalized. I remember thinking that was the worst thing that ever happened. But it was also quite a burden on my mom. He wasn't ever at school. But all of us felt the institutionalization was wrong in one way or another.

Leslie Cohen: We were all really upset he was being institutionalized. We didn't take it out on my mom because she was doing the best she could under the circumstances. She had five kids, my dad had died. We all felt really guilty about him being in an institution, especially a state institution. There was a lot of guilt for my mom. She carried a big load all the time, and wouldn't necessarily let down her guard.

We'd all go down together to visit him at the institution. Very chatty on the way down. We'd go in, it was a dorm situation, and most were retarded. Because no one ever came to see these people, they would just flock around us. At first, it was a little disconcerting because of all these people who looked different. We became better at coping with this as we were more exposed to it. We'd always feel like shit when we left, feel so bad that we had to leave him behind there. We'd also feel bad when we'd show up sometimes and he'd have a bruise and no one knew how it got there. We couldn't get any answers from people. Looking back, I'm kind of wistful, especially because there's so much they're doing with autism now. You kind of wish we could have tried.

Bethany Powers: Emma lived at home until she was 12 or 13. Then she was sent to residential schools in Massachusetts and Pennsylvania until she was 22. I was 9 when Emma went away, and I felt relieved by this. There's bitterness and regret that Emma was sent away, even to this day.

What we did was ultimately bad for Emma. She had a horrible time in the institution she was in. I remember visiting her there; it smelled like an institution – awful. I visited her two times a year at most. Emma was traumatized by this. I don't think she got much of an education in terms of academics. She's bright and could have benefited from education. They did a lot of aversive therapy that has traumatized her to this day. She celebrates every year on the day she was released from this place.

My mother said it [institutionalization] saved her marriage. She feels guilty about it, but she picked her husband and her marriage. I think it was not great, but a good option for the rest of the family at the time. I think it helped all of us. Not Emma, but I don't know what the alternatives were for her of staying in the community. Things are different now. Schools do have facilities.

Group Homes

Olivia Hanover: Matthew didn't go to the group home for five or six years. My mother thought that if she put him there, she was neglecting him and was a horrible mother. They were really hurting him by keeping him home. If they sent him, they felt that they were failing. My grandmother finally said to them, "Are you going to sacrifice four children for the sake of one?"

Jordan Cohen: Marc came home to live in a group home and work in a sheltered workshop. He'd be thrown in and out of community programs because he had behavior problems. He'd bop someone on the head or act out. The ax fell several times: They'd throw him in and throw him out. It gave my mother such heartache. At that time, programs were structured. The person who went into the programs at that time had to fit into the program as it existed. Any deviation, and you were thrown out. It was absolute turmoil.

Lynne Stern Feiges: I always considered us so lucky that Rich was able to live at a group home nearby. All the group home parents throughout the years, as well as his fellow residents, were part of the fabric of our family. We had birthday parties with them. The staff were even seated with my

parents at my wedding. For me, the fact that he was in a community setting (in a house as nice or nicer than ours!) and came home on a regular
basis negated any feelings of isolation from Rich. I never felt badly that he
was out of the house and living there. When he was abruptly discharged
after 25 years, however, I felt extreme loss – as if my family were going
through a divorce or as if the house had burned down or something.
And Rich had no options but to go to an institution for a while. One of
the saddest things was that even if my parents had been capable of living
with him – and they weren't – it would not have been in his best long-
term interest to go live at home. It's true that Rich needs us and we
need him. But he also needs a level of care no one of us is able to provide.

Time-Outs

Sarah Cooper: When he'd be timed-out, we had a broom closet with a
lock outside and a cutout square. He spent most of his life in this closet! Today it would be considered child abuse.

Lynne Stern Feiges: We had this closet in the family room with the bottom
part sawed off. That's where he'd go for time-out. I just accepted this as
his deal, and none of my friends ever said anything when they came over.
Fast-forward 25 years, my parents were househunting and found out that
our old house was on the market. They went in to check it out, and do
you know, that closet was still like that?! Other aversive therapies my parents would tell us not to talk about. There were lots of euphemisms. I
wanted to ask questions, but I couldn't rock the boat too much.

Michael Stern: I saw so many things that I buried deep within my psyche.
I did not talk about it with anyone.

Personal Therapy

Anna Reed: A social worker came from Jewish Social Services and sat us
all down. I remember being bored and doing a somersault off the chair.
The therapist paid attention to me!

Maryann Hall: When she was little I was always jealous because she got to go to therapy and play with these huge balls.

Family Dynamics

The impact of having a family member with a disability is enormous, although highly variable across families. Each family is permanently altered by the presence of the individual with ASD. Many find new meaning and strength in the experience. Other families and marriages falter under the stress. Siblings are generally aware of the strain experienced by their parents, especially when their mothers shouldered the bulk of the burden. As illustrated below, siblings were articulate about both the positive and negative impact their brother or sister's disability had on the family unit.

Accentuating the Positive

Lance Strong: My mom does try to keep it sort of a normal family. In a lot of families with autistic kids, the autistic child becomes the focus of the family and everything in the family revolves around the child. I heard her say that she tries for us not to be a "handicapped" family.

Sarah Cooper: My mother made it extremely manageable for everyone. She didn't make it out to be a problem. It was just a way of life, and it wasn't traumatic. She tried to have a sense of humor about it.

Susan Peters: The strength of my family really influenced the outcome.

Ashley Williams: Todd is almost always included in events. Once my mom and dad and me went to Gettysburg without Todd, and a couple of times we have gone to Illinois by ourselves. Those are the only times we have ever really done something without Todd. There are times we'll go out to dinner or a movie without him, but I feel that's normal for most families. You don't always include everyone.

Jessica Golden: Once Will was in 9th grade, everything was cool again because he had mellowed out. He found his niche of friends – they were the geeks from math and science – and life seemed to be OK.

Dana Peters: Our extended family has been very accepting and supportive. I think it's because of my parents. They saw us accepting it, so they've all been great. We all went back to the Philippines and saw how different it would be if we were living there – in the Philippines, people [with disabilities such as autism] are just sent away.

Lynne Stern Feiges: I am incredibly moved by the loyalty my parents showed for Rich when they were trying to get him out of the institution. They fought for him to get out of there with every fiber of their being, going to see him practically every day and talking to anyone who would listen. It was truly breathtaking. My mom especially – what an example of parental dedication. I think I knew this before, but now I had a chance to really see it. If it weren't for Rich, maybe I would not have understood this so deeply.

Jordan Cohen: My dad had a very strong bond with Marc. Before the advent of special education, Marc was never the beneficiary of any public education, so my dad taught him. He taught him how to read by using the *TV Guide* – he was so into television. Dad was probably closer to Marc than any of us.

Family Stress and Marital Strife

Becky Lott: My mom says she doesn't know if she could ever go through it again. It was hard on her, and she did everything for him. My dad didn't acknowledge it as much as my mother did. She talks to me about this now.

Jessica Golden: My mother never blamed Will, but it was a very big stress on the family dynamic. My younger brother had medical problems, too. My dad said one day that he couldn't deal with it any more. Then he got up and left. My mom said it was hard for him to deal with. You go to family outings and people are like, can't you control your kid? My mom said my dad couldn't handle Will because he saw some of himself in him. To me, Will's presence had a lot more impact than on my younger brother, who always lived with it. He didn't have the before and after effect, so it was no big deal.

Sarah Cooper: My parents were married out of high school, then they had me. Children raising children! Add an autistic child into the equation, and it gets a little tricky. My parents' marriage suffered (after the diagnosis). Rick wasn't to blame for the divorce, but it certainly didn't help. Some people get it and some don't. It was a lot easier for us to manage and get through the day with my father out of the picture.

Anna Reed: I thought that if I could just get everybody doing the right things, that he would be OK. That if my father would just soften up and my mother just stop protecting him, then we would get his behavior in line.

Bethany Powers: My father was full of rage and anguish, my mother said, and could not cope on a day-to-day basis with Emma in his life. My father still can't see how wonderful Emma is. Instead, he focuses on all the little ways in which she has failed. They have a very troubled relationship that is nonetheless very close.

When she left, there was relief but, on the one hand, also tremendous guilt. My parents drove her to the school and came back. My dad was thirsty and drank some lemonade my mother made, and it wasn't sweet enough. He started putting in sugar, more sugar, more sugar, and then the phone rang. It was the principal of Emma's old school, and my mother told him that my father's drink was three quarters full with sugar and still not sweet enough for him. The principal was a diabetic and told my mother to get my father to the hospital right away, that this was diabetes. Generally, diabetes creeps up on you. My father, that day, was diagnosed with the most serious form of diabetes. Within weeks, he was insulin dependent. I believe that my father's body shut down and that he tried to die that day. Somewhere deep inside of himself the pain over giving up on my sister – his relief – nearly destroyed him and killed him. It was an amazing thing to have happened right then.

Sam Cohen: We were kind of the black sheep on my mother's side of the family. It was all rough, and Marc was one other thing to prove to them that we weren't as good as them – at least that's how I felt.

Inequities

The reality of life in families with a member who has a developmental disability is that siblings are treated differently. No matter how hard they try to be fair, parents must adapt to the needs and capacities of the child with the disability in a number of ways. Some of these accommodations create feelings of resentment in typical siblings. One particularly sore spot for typical siblings is the management of behaviors that are clearly unacceptable, yet somehow sanctioned if displayed by the child with ASD.

Inequities in expectations for family participation also breeds resentment. Most of the typical siblings expressed some bittersweet feelings about their own successes, for instance. They were acutely aware of the pain their parents might feel when recognizing that the child with ASD would not be able to experience the developmental transitions or successes that defined the lives of their typical children.

Setting Standards

Jessica Golden: To this day, I feel my mother has different standards for him. She let him live with her and didn't make him pay rent. She uses excuses for him, like "Will doesn't have money for this or that." I'm like, he has a job – but, I never needed the help. I feel he had it hard, but my mom made excuses. It was always, "Poor Will." I was like, well maybe he should get help. Instead of, say, failing a class, maybe he should do something about it. The answer was always, "Well, you know Will." He always refused help because he didn't want to admit he had a disability.

Becky Lott: We were all treated equally. Gordon never bothered me. Now my younger brother, we still fight!

Ashley Williams: I never felt that I was treated different than Todd. We were both basically raised and treated the same way.

Lynne Stern Feiges: I never felt there was intentional inequity from my parents. The most I can say is that it is perhaps a shame Rich took up so much of their emotional energy. A friend told me recently that it is easier for me because the profound nature of Rich's disability makes things cut and dry, as opposed to his siblings, who have pathologies that are significant and disruptive but "under other people's radar." I have to agree. It is so obvious to me how great Rich's needs are, I would consider myself a bad person to be jealous of the attention he received from my parents.

Normalizing the Abnormal

Jessica Golden: We used to go to synagogue and Will would have a tantrum. He'd call my mother "Nancy," not "mom." My mom wouldn't care, but my grandmother would say, "It's OK, it's OK, it's really not strange because it's part of his program." Everyone was trying to pretend that what was abnormal was normal, especially my grandmother.

Anna Reed: Recently, Joseph exhibited some bad social behavior where I would have thought, had I not been diagnosing him recently, he's just an asshole. Instead, I decided to just interpret it differently as ... he really doesn't know social skills because of his disability. But mom won't acknowledge this. She always just rationalizes what he does. A couple of years ago this upset me, but now I try to think, OK, she needs to grieve the fact that she has a handicapped son. It's 40 years later, but I need to keep telling her this is how I feel.

Selective Functioning by Sibling with ASD

Jessica Golden: It sounds very petty, because I know he's overwhelmed, but he breaks commitments. For instance, he forgot my mom and grandparents' holiday party. I had to go, but he doesn't. I confront him on this. We're always doing things for the family, but Will gets out of it all the time. He says he can't be bothered with it all. All my life, I feel like Will gets out of things because he had a problem. I'm not negating that, but he still doesn't get it, and it completely infuriates me. I don't know if he's selective about things. I mean, he holds down a job, so ... I've had this issue for a very long time. It's kind of neat in a way, because we do have a "regular" sibling relationship.

Burden of Extra Chores

Julie Shore: I do all the chores. I have to work for that little brat! I refer to him like that because he gets away with murder. He'll kick me and fall down purposefully and yell "ow!" He makes the chores by knocking down all the books on a shelf, and then it's easier for me to pick them up.

Maryann Hall: I wish I could have a sister that's normal because I have to always do all the work. My parents blame stuff on me and they say she doesn't understand. But I think she does understand, and it makes me feel bad because I always have to take the blame. My sister hardly does any chores around the house, and I have to do a lot. It makes it unfair for me.

Less Attention

Julie Shore: I don't try to be the "good child" because I don't think it's fair that he gets all the attention. He knows what he's doing. He's being manipulative and getting exactly what he wants because he realizes he has an excuse. I'm not gonna be the kid who sits there and won't say anything and doesn't deal with my problems because of him!

Anna Reed: Joseph's social skills are really poor, and it infuriates me that they get locked into this thing where my mother overcaters to him and my dad does the reverse, thinking he's just a spoiled brat. As if he's NOT disabled! My mother's pretty obsessed with Joseph. He will interrupt, so no matter what, if he starts talking, that's where the attention goes.

Michael Stern: I didn't perceive any inequality growing up. However, it became more and more apparent over time that my parents devoted most of their emotional energies to Rich. At times I grew resentful of this. Rich seemed to bring out a softer, more maternal side of my mother that she rarely showed to us growing up.

Tempered Success

Anna Reed: There is huge guilt I have about being successful in areas and enjoying positive things because it was always like "isn't it nice I can do that but he can't." My mother, I know, has always felt sad about it, and it made me so sad. I see her sorrow when I get things that he can't. And it makes me feel really mixed about my successes.

Living with Behavior Problems

By far, one of the greatest sources of stress reported by our respondents was living with challenging behaviors. Behavioral difficulties created family disruptions, fear, and embarrassment. The more unpredictable the behavioral escalations were, the more difficult it was for typical siblings to relax and feel comfortable in their families. Indeed, the presence of severe behaviors curtailed the degree to which typical siblings could experience normative events (vacations, outings, etc.). Obsessive, rigid, or ritualistic behavior also created vivid memories for siblings, who were often perplexed and annoyed by them.

Unpredictable Behaviors

Jamie Cohen: When he was thrown out of a program, he couldn't understand why he couldn't go there every day. He got very upset to the point of being violent and ramming his hand through a glass window and kicking my mom across the room. The frustration had never come out in that manner before. I remember him saying that he didn't mean it, or something to that effect. It was the first time I'd ever heard him talking what would be considered normally. That much frustration got his communication to what we'd consider a normal level.

Olivia Hanover: Matthew used to bang holes in the walls. He couldn't help it. We just patched 'em up! It took a toll.

Becky Lott: In some ways it was hard because we never got to go on vacation. Gordon doesn't like crowds and or being around a lot of people. So, he'd have tantrums if there were people around him.

Richard Flynn: Sometimes I wish David wasn't autistic so he'd be able to talk; and so he wouldn't bite and scratch.

Jeremy Plant: Sometimes he can be the greatest kid around, and sometimes he's a little monster. In the past, he would pinch and bite me. He is almost fearful of me now. He won't do that stuff. When I scold him and tell him not to act a certain way, he stops.

Anna Reed: By the time I was in 5th grade, my mother was working with my dad at his office. Joseph got angry at me and my other brother, took scissors, and threatened everyone. I locked myself in my parents' bedroom, called my mother at work, and made her promise she would take him to counseling the next day.

Leslie Cohen: One time he had an episode where he was screaming and yelling and I had to hold him down. All of a sudden he said something rational, and we were like, "whoa, that's weird."

Julie Shore: When he comes into my room, I kick him out. I yell, "Robby!" and he runs out. He knows he's not welcome. I don't like him in my room because he likes to knock down a lot of my books. There aren't too many places we can take him without him going ballistic. MacDonald's is fine, though, because he knows he's getting french fries! We can't take him anywhere without fries!

Jordan Cohen: We never left the house as a full family to do anything. We never went out to dinner because someone always had to be home with Marc. There was a real feeling of isolation from everyone. I don't think there was ever any resentment, though. If there was any, it went toward my extended family, which never helped with my [ailing] grandmother.

Olivia Hanover: You couldn't go out as a family. Everything had to be prioritized around Matthew. It was like, "OK, we're going to the beach, who is watching Matthew?"

Maryann Hall: I wish we could shop or watch movies together. Sometimes we all eat together or we'll go out to the "Y."

Dana Peters: Growing up, we didn't go out much. We went to church together. Getting him to sit through an hour was an arduous task.

When I left home for school, I remember Chris didn't understand where I was going. When they dropped me off at school – which was only about 10 minutes away – he'd try to pull me into the car and say, "Let's go home, let's go home." He didn't understand, but he knew something had changed. My mom helped me pack up my room, and he'd try to unpack everything. After I went away, he wouldn't come in my room. But by the time my sister went to school, he understood she was coming back.

Sam Cohen: Marc scares my 4-year-old daughter every once in a while. I tell her he's special and hasn't grown up. Things she can understand. There are times she tells me she doesn't want him to come over. I'll say, "Honey, we're his family and we have to take care of him." She'll accept that. But he'll do things that really frighten her like inhale food until he gets sick. He threw up, and it just freaked her out.

Obsessive Behaviors

Jessica Golden: Will talked very little, but maps, he could tell you how to get from here to Los Angeles! Then, he'd make maps on the carpet, making roads with his finger. If you'd step on them, he'd scream. If you were driving and the car didn't stay in the same lane, that would completely make him go nuts.

Bethany Powers: Emma would listen to loud rock music with headphones. She would rock constantly, and it was distressing to see her there in the rocking chair rocking steadily and tuning out the rest of the world.

Ashley Williams: Todd seems to know exactly what buttons to push on me (good or bad) to make me do what he wants. If he wants me to play with him, he'll keep hugging me or give me a kiss until I do. Sometimes he is just like a normal sibling that wants to bug his sister. It's like he knows I want to be alone, and he'll constantly be around me or he'll do the one thing that bothers me most.

Susan Peters: Chris went through phases where he would tantrum and not eat normal food. Once he would only eat chicken from Roy Rogers.

Dana Peters: When he was little, he didn't like putting his clothes on. So, he'd just run around the house in his diapers.

Jordan Cohen: There were odd behavior patterns. He'd only eat certain things: oatmeal or spaghetti. If you tried to feed him something else, he wouldn't eat it. Marc kind of languished at home. We would chain him in the house so he couldn't get out. He wasn't toilet trained until he was 9.

Lance Strong: He hums and recites stories off his videotapes. At the dinner table, we say, "shh" and "stop." Sometimes he'll stop for a second, but then he keeps on going. If he doesn't stop, we just wait it out because there's no point in going after him and after him and after him if he's not gonna stop. He's got a huge bag of videos. I don't like 'em all. I wish he was into books or something a little more quiet. He hums loudly a lot.

Growing Up

One of the most profound realities of life with a sibling with ASD is that normative transitions, such as going to school together or playing in sports leagues together, do not occur. Alternately, a normative transition may be available only to one sibling in that one sibling achieves independent adulthood, while the other may need support and assistance mostly associated with youth. In fact, it is sometimes hard for the family to define the individual with ASD as an adult at all, as they may continue to perceive him or her as a child.

As adulthood comes for the typical sibling, there is usually a very definitive shift in the relationship between siblings. For example, the typical sibling may feel greater responsibility. The sibling relationship may also become more complex if, for example, the typical sibling moves away and becomes less aware of the details of the daily life of the sibling with ASD. Many of these siblings' comments reflect the complex nature of the sibling relationship as time goes on.

Sam Cohen: I'll make the connection every once in a while that I'm talking to Marc like I talk to my 4-year-old. And I'll use the same words or tone of voice. It feels odd.

Sarah Cooper: One thing I struggle with today is that I feel almost more like a mother than I do a sister. I think my relationship with Rick is very complex because I feel like a mother, sister, therapist, friend, nurse. That becomes extremely emotional. I'm always helping him with something.

Maryann Hall: I help my mom and sister a lot. When we go swimming, I help get her towel ready, and I help put her clothes on, and I lay everything out for her. I have to act like the big sister, even though I am not.

Lynne Stern Feiges: Rich will be 60 years old, and I'll still think of him as my little brother. When he was hospitalized last summer, for the first few days and weeks we were all on a mad search for information. We made calls and researched programs and medicine that could possibly help him. There were a thousand messages on each other's voicemail. All of a sudden, my mom leaves me a message saying that we all don't realize it, but we are researching programs for children even though Rich is an adult. I wouldn't even have caught that, but it was true. I was having hour-long conversations with people about children's psychiatric hospitals and whatnot without realizing that these places no longer applied to Rich because he was an adult. It was astonishing, really. We all just think of him as a little boy.

Jordan Cohen: When Marc got his own apartment, we had a huge party. I registered him at a department store, like a bride, and sent out a couple of hundred invitations. Hired a band. The next day, my mom got sick and she died of heart failure a few days later. Her last question to me was whether Marc would be OK. All she ever wanted was for him to be safe and near.

There were times when I was the only one left in town that I felt resentment toward my siblings. During a crisis period when Marc was without services, I'd ask for help from my brother and be told that he had his own family, that this was my responsibility, etc. I told him I resented him. When my mom died, however, Sam emerged as a wonderful support for Marc. He takes him to his house almost every weekend. They take good care of him.

Jessica Golden: Still to this day, Will always gets mad because he is in competition with my younger brother, who is smarter and makes more money and always seems to win, especially with girls. Will feels in competition with the two of us and always tracks our progress. He made a comment to me about a year ago, saying that I was lucky because I was smart, and that he always had to work hard, etc., etc. That annoys me.

Situations and Solutions

◆ The **road to a correct diagnosis** can be long and confusing for both parents and siblings. Things may even be
complicated by a child's regression after seemingly typical
development. Siblings perceive and often internalize this
struggle within the family, even though parents do not
directly involve them in it. On the other hand, some siblings feel relief at being kept out of things and allowed to
"just be a kid."

Part of being a parent involves knowing what each
child in the family needs and benefits from. Parents who
monitor their young typical child's reactions to information and involvement will be able to match the child's
interest and tolerance levels. Older siblings should be
encouraged to communicate clearly about how much
involvement they desire, so that the level of involvement
is comfortable to them.

◆ Parents often **explain ASD to siblings** by telling them
that their brother or sister is and will be "different." Siblings
can use this idea to find a sense of normalcy even when
the family dynamic is rife with unpredictable events and
behaviors. Nearly all children can understand difference
as it relates to more obvious disabilities. For example,
people need glasses because they can't see well, some
people can't hear well and therefore need a hearing aid,
some people need to use a wheelchair, and so on.

Parents can take this understanding to a new level by
explaining that some people have trouble with things
that you cannot see so easily. It is also helpful to point
out that everyone has trouble with something. For
example, a typical sibling might have difficulty with math
or might need special help with reading. An analogy can
then be drawn to difficulties a person with ASD has –

perhaps in talking, in following the rules of a game, in making friends, or in understanding jokes. Whenever the concept of difference is explained, it is important to stress how the individual with ASD is the same as other children or the child spoken to in most other respects. That is, children with ASD, just like typical children, have preferences for toys, movies, TV, shoes, animals, computer games, and so on. These similarities should not be obscured in a discussion of difference.

◆ Having a sibling with ASD in a family with just two children can be extremely disappointing for the typically developing child, who may regret **not having a companion** within the family. But this is not always the case. Some siblings perceive this circumstance as an opportunity for personal growth.

For the typical sibling in this circumstance, it is especially important that parents ensure that he or she is not overwhelmed with expectations of success. (Some feel they must succeed exceptionally, given the sibling's disability.) Thus, siblings must be reminded that they are not responsible for the family's success or happiness, which depends much more on things such as marital harmony, financial stability, and good health.

◆ Siblings may secretly harbor a sense of responsibility for or guilt about their brother or sister's ASD by associating **physical aggression** they may have shown toward their sibling as the "cause" of the disorder.

It is important to help siblings understand that such interactions cannot cause ASD. Encouraging them to speak openly to a supportive person might help ease these negative feelings or fears. Even just knowing that such feelings are common among people in this circumstance can help reduce feelings of isolation for the typical sibling.

◆ Even though a typical sibling may understand her high-functioning brother or sister's limitations, resentment may develop if parents hold **different standards** for their children in terms of family obligations or financial responsibilities.

Siblings need to understand that negative feelings are acceptable. While most siblings demonstrate tremendous love and compassion for their brother or sister with ASD, they are only human! The complexity of the situation demands a tolerance for feelings of all kinds. When siblings can acknowledge some of those feelings, which may include shame, guilt, or intense anger, they are often able to move beyond them.

Many typical siblings struggle with understanding how their sibling with ASD can function so effectively in some contexts and not in others. For example, a sibling with ASD may be a model citizen at school but truly destructive at home. Similarly, a high-functioning sibling with ASD may be able to get a graduate degree, but will fail to remember an important family event. While this **apparent "selectivity"** may seem intentional, in fact, it usually simply reflects the core deficits of ASD: People with ASD do not perceive the social cues and conventions that govern the behavior of most others. It is helpful for the typical sibling to remember this in times of frustration.

◆ Younger siblings may feel like their brother or sister with ASD is being manipulative by destroying objects that belong to the typical sibling. **Establishing boundaries**, such as keeping a lock on a bedroom door, may help a typical sibling feel less threatened. Typical siblings are entitled to feel safe, to be able to keep their things out of harm's way, and to have a place that is their own. There should be a balance between what one gives to others in the family and what one does and needs for oneself. Parents must take the lead in this regard and strongly support the separate needs of the typical siblings. This may take the form of giving consequences to the sibling with ASD when he or she engages in destructive behavior or helping the typical sibling to find safe areas for prized possessions.

◆ The **eldest sibling may disconnect** from others in the family by developing an active life of his or her own. This can lead to a sense of relief or guilt on the older sibling's part and resentment from the younger typically developing siblings in the family. Siblings closer in age to their brother or sister with ASD report feeling more impacted by the disability. Conversely, some older siblings report being affected by the "before and after" effect that younger siblings do not experience because they have always had a brother or sister with ASD.

Birth order and age spacing have an impact on the extent to which siblings feel affected by the presence of ASD in the family. However, it is important not to over-generalize in this area. Many other more relevant aspects of family life affect a sibling's adjustment, most notably parental adaptation, coping, and communication. It is helpful for parents to be mindful of equity in the provision of assistance and support. Even when there is a very willing member of the family, it is important that no one member is overburdened with responsibility. It is also important for the family to reach solutions that require the cooperation and participation of everybody, in whatever individualized ways are palatable and functional.

◆ Siblings generally are very **sensitive to the welfare of their brother or sister**, even if parents do not openly share their trials and tribulations. Many siblings are very attuned to the experiences of their sibling with ASD and to the family's concerns, attending to nuances of interaction and circumstance.

Open lines of communication between parents and typically developing siblings help a great deal by allowing siblings to understand that their parents are struggling, too. When siblings are children, it is the parents' responsibility to monitor their adjustment, to shield them from unnecessary worry, to involve them as appropriate, and to explain as needed. Most important, it is parents' responsibility to allow siblings to have and to express a wide range of feelings. It is natural for siblings to sometimes feel negatively toward their sibling with a disability, and it is important that parents allow the typical sibling to have and to share those feelings. When such feelings can be dealt with honestly and lovingly, the likelihood of unspoken resentment or wracking guilt is minimized. While it can be difficult for parents to tolerate the expression of such feelings, it is important for the health of the family and the emotional well-being of the sibling that open expression of feelings is not thwarted.

When siblings are adults, their relationship with parents may become more reciprocal. That is, an adult child may transition into checking on the emotional well-being of an aging parent and can provide support regarding worries over the family member with ASD. This is an extension of the type of caretaking that characterizes adult children's relationships with aging parents in typical families.

◆ Many siblings do not **talk about their brother or sister's ASD** with friends, except when asked. Sometimes such reticence results from an inability to articulate the nature or consequences of autism. At other times, a profound sense of embarrassment prevents them from speaking more openly about their sibling with a disability. In any case, a closed stance leads to isolation and to avoidance of social circumstances and, therefore, should be avoided, if at all possible.

Helping the typical sibling to explain ASD releases him or her from secrecy and shame. (See suggestions in Appendix B.) Sometimes, portrayals of people with ASD in the media provide a sense of relief for siblings, who can then use these depictions to explain their brother or sister's condition to others. Often, elementary, middle, and high school children are helped by being involved in a sibling support group, which provides a unique opportunity for reducing isolation and a forum for discussing issues such as explaining ASD to others. While sibling support groups are not available in all areas of the country, online (see Appendix C), or pen pal resources might serve a similar function. Also, a specialized school program might be willing to host a special siblings day or an informative workshop to address these concerns.

◆ Siblings appreciate a parent's attempt to **avoid becoming a "handicapped" family**, in which the child with ASD is the constant focus. This can be difficult, however, in light of the day-to-day realities of having a member of the family with ASD. Siblings must feel entitled to lead normal lives of their own and have typical family experiences. While being a sibling of a person with ASD is life-altering, it need not be the entire identity of a sibling.

Families address this issue in a variety of unique and creative ways. There may be activities that include the individual with ASD and activities that are conducted separately. Or, parents might split activities to be able to give more individual attention to each child at times. Again, balance is preferable. It is not advisable for a family to allow the typical sibling to avoid engaging in activities with the individual with ASD. In that atmosphere, it is hard to create a family context, as there is little opportunity for cohesion or even for shared experience and memories.

◆ At family gatherings, **extended family members may learn to accept** the sibling with ASD and show support when parents and other siblings demonstrate their own acceptance of the situation.

People take their cues from those who live with the person with ASD. When family members communicate and demonstrate acceptance, the likelihood of larger-scale acceptance increases. The way in which this is done varies by family, and by the individual with ASD. Examples include having a confirmation or bar mitzvah for a sibling with ASD, or including him or her in a wedding reception line. Such public display of inclusion not only facilitates the broader acceptance of the person with ASD, but also serves to integrate him or her into the extended family.

◆ **Residential placement** may provide relief to a family (and a marriage), but may also induce tremendous guilt, especially if the placement is less than optimal. This was true for many families who faced institutionalization in the 1960s and '70s, but is also true now with regard to community placements. Such decisions always bring a mixture of feelings, all of which are legitimate. Typical siblings will always feel a sense of sadness that their brother or sister is not afforded the same amount of opportunities or choices that they are. This is part of the reality of the awareness they carry with them.

Chapter 3

A Sense of Responsibility: Getting and Staying Involved

Having a sibling with special needs almost inevitably results in increased responsibility for typical siblings. It is not surprising, therefore, that the theme of responsibility emerged over and over again in our interviews. Siblings described themselves as helpers, mentors and, sometimes, substitute parents for their siblings with ASD. Even from young ages, typical siblings expressed a sense of being a source of comfort to their brother or sister with ASD. Additionally, siblings felt globally responsible for their parents' emotional state, for their family's well-being, and for the future, including ensuring fair treatment and safety of their brother or sister.

In this chapter, we will examine the multiple ways in which a typical sibling feels responsible for a brother or sister with ASD. We will also explore how this sense of responsibility affects the typical sibling emotionally.

Siblings as Teachers

Although it is crucial for parents to protect their typical children from premature adult responsibilities, siblings can fulfill a valuable mentoring role toward their brother or sister with ASD. Siblings in our interviews who took the time and had the patience for their special sibling found a sense of fulfillment and connection; and, many times, these efforts also felt rewarding.

Richard Flynn: I try to teach him how to say some things. He never says anything I ask him to. I'll hold his hand if he needs to get his diaper changed.

Jeremy Plant: I worry people will take advantage of him when he's older. Right now we're trying to teach him the concept of money. Like three ones aren't better than a 20, etc. I don't want someone jippin' him.

Sarah Cooper: I was never called on to step in and do things, but I always watched Rick. "Don't do this, watch out, sit over here," that sort of thing. Rick came home every other weekend. I was the watcher. He went everywhere with us. He loves to eat, so we'd go food shopping.

"Parentification"

One way in which responsibility sometimes manifests is in the concept of parentification. In other words, siblings sometimes take on roles and responsibilities that are otherwise charged to parents. At times, a par-entified role is a chosen one, one that the person feels comfortable inhabiting. In some cases, a parentified role goes along with a desire to protect the parents from the reality of the situation. At other times, the parentified role is thrust upon the sibling without notice or assent. In such circumstances some siblings have strong feelings of anger or of abandonment, as they helplessly watch their parents refuse to manage the situation or plan for the future appropriately.

Our interviews illustrate the siblings' concern for their brothers and sisters, regardless of the paths to these positions. Some siblings were amazed at how much responsibility they had assumed, others were amazed that they had been permitted to assume so much responsibility. Listen as they share their stories of struggle and of pride.

Voluntary

Sarah Cooper: My mother went to Singapore, and I took over responsibilities for Rick. We made a room for him, and my husband was really patient about it. I was a little nervous with my mom out of the country, but I enjoyed it and it wasn't altogether that different. When she came back, it was almost like she was invading my space.

Until recently, my dad would call and say, "How's Rick? Is he getting any better?" That was always hard to take. Finally, I'd say, "No, he's not. This is it." My dad comes out once a year and watches Rick then. But that's about it. I accept it. My dad's a good father with Rick. They go to Six Flags Great Adventure. He just can't live with him. I get nervous when dad comes out because Rick has a lot of seizures. It's really bad, he bites his tongue ... pure hell ... and I don't want my father seeing that. I just don't. I don't want him to feel terribly guilty, and I don't want him to panic, because it's shocking. I want to be there if something happens. Not that I don't think he can handle it; I just feel the need to be there. Rick is not just my mother's responsibility; he's everybody's.

Susan Peters: I don't think my parents put pressure on me. I put the responsibility on myself. I was trying to understand it emotionally, and I felt that I needed to be there for him. I'm not sure of the reasons. Looking back, I think it might have been too much because it was harder for me. I was really shy when I was younger, so it was easy for me to escape, having a brother with needs. I was quick to help out more because I was shy.

Leslie Cohen: It's a parental type of thing because I'm always concerned for him. With another sibling you hope they can take care of themselves by the time they're in their 40s or so! We all constantly worry about him, whether he'll be OK and whether others will get threatened by his size. You hope he doesn't get thrown out of a program and you'll have to start at ground zero again.

Involuntary

Anna Reed: For years I worked on them [my parents] getting a will together, which they put off because they couldn't figure out what to do with Joseph. I sent them information and names to contact and they wouldn't follow through. They somehow got it together when my dad got cancer.

For years my big thing was for them to help him learn independent skills and move out of the house. My father would occasionally blow up at him, saying, "he should move the hell out of here," as if he were just a rotten kid. And, my mother, meanwhile, is packing his lunches and doing everything for him and just babying his temper tantrums. I recently downloaded some information about planning after parents die and had them read it. I was begging my mother to just have a discussion with him and offer him the option of moving out before they die so that they could help him become independent. I said to them, if you don't do it, you're telling me I have to do it.

Gradually, I'm letting go of feeling so badly that my parents don't get to live alone without Joseph in the house. For many years, I saw it as my path to get into these long conversations with my parents about how they can help him move out. They have now accepted this, so the burden has been lifted off me a little. I'm still trying for the future planning for him. I am feeling a little less responsible for it now. It's ridiculous that I took so much responsibility. But also that they let me!

Olivia Hanover: A lot of responsibility was thrust on us [for him and for ourselves] because his needs were primary. For instance, I wanted to work in high school and I couldn't because my mother couldn't pick me up. I had to be there for support of my mother because my dad traveled a lot. So as the daughter and the only girl, a lot of responsibility fell in my lap. That was the way it went, and it made me a better person with a greater understanding of what my parents went through.

Bethany Powers: About 10 years ago, my parents started going to Florida for the winter. The first winter, they said, "Oh, and Emma will be fine, give her a call from time to time." At this point, Emma and I had a relationship where I only saw her at family parties. I was ashamed of her still. Maybe once a year, she and I would go out and do something together. I've come to terms with their doing this. They were completely wrong. I didn't recognize this as my parents abdicating their responsibility for several years. They went off to Florida, and Emma felt abandoned. She had a terrible winter, unable to sleep, fearful. She called me and said kids were teasing her and asked to stay with me. At the time I thought that I had to cope with the situation right now. I brought her back, and realized there was no way the teasing was actually happening, given her apartment location and the cold that winter. She was probably having hallucinations and fears. We were both up all night, and I was petrified because I felt like this enormous weight of responsibility had landed solely on me. I was single, knew my sister little, and didn't know what to do.

What followed was a period of years where I took over more and more of the responsibility for Emma because I felt that if I didn't she would drop through the cracks. My parents had stopped. I went to therapy. I was angry, I was too scared. I unloaded everything on the therapist, and the place that I ended up was that if I didn't come to terms with my sister, nothing else in my life would ever work. I knew that was a fact that went deeper than worrying about the responsibility or thinking that this was unfair. This had to do with central questions of identification for me. This was mine: it was my sister and this was about me. I didn't have to pick her up — many people would have walked away. That choice was mine. So, I chose to build a relationship with my sister and I know I did the right thing. I could not have lived with myself otherwise.

Acceptance

A certain grace permeates many of the siblings' responses about their responsibility for the future of their sibling with ASD. Acceptance of the reality of their sibling's needs and of their own position and obligation to assist is a prominent theme.

Jeremy Plant: I've told them over and over that when I get my own place, if he were living in some crummy group home, I'd get him out of there. I have a feeling that somewhere down the road, I'll be his main caretaker. I've thought of this since age 16. It doesn't bother me; he's my only brother.

My mom has always told me I shouldn't be the one taking care of him but I'm thinking, who else is there to do it? Other people tell me that I do a lot of good things for him, and I'm not even his parent. I say, "Yeah, well, someone's got to do something!"

Becky Lott: If he has to live with me, he has to live with me. He's my brother, and I have to do whatever I can for him.

Dana Peters: I've tried to get everyone to talk about the details of what will happen, but it's hard to broach that topic because it's assuming certain details of what will happen. My parents asked us recently about making us Chris' guardians. It was sad to talk about it. There's so many "what ifs." I think they're worried also.

Michael Stern: I worry very much about Rich's future, especially when my parents can't care for him any longer. That is why we've decided to remain in the state so we can be physically close by when needed one day. I do feel that it's my duty to carry on for them once they no longer can. This is very important to them. I want them to be comforted that Rich will be taken care of by us.

Sarah Cooper: There was an underlying sense of pity for me from my relatives. There was a lot of whispering. They'd always say that I was such a good sister – which became condescending. I'm like, well, I don't have a choice.

Approaches to the Future

Each family deals with planning for the future of the child with ASD in a unique way. Solutions reflect the roles traditionally assumed by different members of the family, the personalities of each sibling, and each person's comfort level as they anticipate playing a significant role in the life of their sibling with a disability. Some siblings find peace in being the involved member, while others find solace in keeping some distance, in normalizing a low level of contact, or in emphasizing the positive aspects of their sibling's life.

Anna Reed: I talked with my other siblings. My older brother is sort of the absent-minded professor, off studying as long as I can remember. He's gotten away. My youngest brother – he's financially better off – will end up taking a lot of the responsibility. I have less patience and tolerance for Joseph's social skills stuff. It grosses me out more, his table manners and stuff. I can't even stand to sit next to him.

Sam Cohen: Regarding the future, I don't feel a whole lot of responsibility. Legally, Jamie is his guardian, and I know Jordan is so devoted to him. Nothin' bad is gonna happen to him. When we're all gone, he'll still be around! He's not going to be homeless or want for anything.

Lance Strong: The way that people's brothers or sisters aren't really in their lives when they go off to college and get a job somewhere else; they don't see them except at family gatherings. The future will be pretty much like that.

Julie Shore: I'm hoping when he gets older he'll be able to go to a group home, not an institution or anything. I'm not gonna let him in one of those places. I'll sue them if they do any of the bad things I've heard happen in institutions. I'd like to be able to check up on him every two weeks or once a month, to make sure he's OK, making progress, and no one is feeding him rubber gloves! I wish that he could be independent, but I don't really see that too much.

Ashley Williams: I constantly feel responsible for Todd and his future. I mean, I am his sister and everything; I'm supposed to be responsible for him. I do at times have worries that when Todd is an adult and my parents are dead and I'm away somewhere, that there's going to be no one to watch or guard the people who are taking care of Todd. I'll hopefully be able to handle the situation when it presents itself.

Jordan Cohen: It's not so much that there will ever be a cure. The reality is to make life as productive as possible for Marc, rather than trying to cure him – because you can't cure him. You basically learn to make life as enjoyable as you can, and I think he does have an enjoyable life ... the fact that he is out of the institution.

Regarding the Outside World

The theme of responsibility is also played out in the realm of the social world outside of the family. The excerpts below illustrate how a sense of responsibility toward a brother or sister with ASD led some siblings to take unusual roles socially or mold their lives in a certain way.

Jessica Golden: When I was in 6th grade and he was in 3rd, Will was mainstreamed completely into elementary school. He must have had a tantrum [one day] and the teachers came to me, as a sister, and said your brother's doing whatever. They pulled me out of class and asked me to help them out. I remember going there and telling him to stop. As a teacher, this is unbelievable to me. But, on the other hand, they probably didn't know what else to do. In retrospect, I think maybe they didn't have any support in the program. This was the late '70s and they probably had never seen an autistic kid in their entire life. They never got me again because I think my mother called!

Lynne Stern Feiges: In my senior year of college, I had to make a decision about graduate school. I had majored in psychology and always toyed with the idea of becoming a therapist, special ed teacher, or something like that. But I also wanted to go to law school – this had been a secret goal of mine since I was younger. I remember feeling this sense that I "should" go the therapist route. And, I think now that this was rooted in a sense of responsibility that somehow I had to add to the field that would help my brother. I talked about my quandary with Rich's then-house parent. She heard me out and then said, "Lynne, go to law school, you've already lived this." That was it for me – I eventually went to law school.

Susan Peters: It was different for me than it was for Dana. It had more of an impact on me in terms of the responsibility I took on doing day-to-day stuff or on the weekends. I'd volunteer more than my sister. I think Chris and I had more of a connection because of our closeness in age. The clinicians asked me to help out because they could see how he responded to me.

Effects of Increased Responsibility

One of the consequences of feeling responsible for a sibling in multiple ways is stress. Just as each sibling navigates the role of sibling uniquely, each experiences stress in unique ways. Even as children, some siblings internalize parental fears and feel burdened either by caretaking duties or by a vague sense of being "older than one's years." Other siblings may wonder as children whether they could have done something to prevent a behavioral outburst, taking the sense of responsibility to a new level. Still other siblings experience ambivalence or guilt over the extent to which they should plan a "separate" future versus how much they should consider their sibling's needs in making their own life plans.

Jeremy Plant: My mom is fearful of what's going to happen with him. She's always been fearful of what happens when I can't take care of him. That happened in November; she institutionalized him. I wasn't happy about that, and we didn't speak for more than a month afterward. I didn't think there was a need for it. Then again, I'm not with him 24/7.

Maryann Hall: The worst part is doing all the work and always taking care of her. I tell my parents, "She's not my child and I don't have to help her."

Dana Peters: It was kind of a drag going to family parties because some-one always had to be with Chris. My sister and I had to take turns watching him. How can you play with the other kids when you're hang-ing out with your little brother?

I go through waves now where I think about it all the time. We think about what will happen when my parents are not around. Even moving to Boston was a huge deal for me. It was hard because I didn't want my parents to think I was shunning all responsibility; but there's this sense in me that inevitably I'll have to go back there. I had a much harder time picking up and moving than other people would because I had that [sibling responsibilities] at home.

My sister and I have said often that we have to be in the tri-state area. It's nice because I know my sister and I are both there. I really love it here [in Boston], but at the same time, that scares me because I don't want to get too attached to some place I have to leave. His entire life is there.

Susan Peters: When I was younger and saw my brother upset, tantruming, or out of control, I kind of wondered if there was something that I did — because he couldn't express what was bothering him. I never felt responsible for the autism, though.

Jordan Cohen: I always felt like a missionary. Like there was a responsibility that I had to do something for Marc and, further, for other people like him.

Jamie Cohen: I remember as a teenager always feeling responsible or older than I was.

Situations and Solutions

◆ One of the ways in which siblings take responsibility for their brother or sister with a disability is by **teaching life skills**, such as learning the value of money. Some do this out of a sense of worry that others will take advantage of their brother or sister. Others try to help prepare their sibling for the larger world, in whatever small and concrete ways they can.

  The role of teacher is a special way to support a sibling in meeting the challenges of living more independently. It is a way to facilitate a sibling's growth, to assume a mentoring role with the sibling, and to assist parents in preparing their child with ASD for life beyond childhood. Some individuals with ASD carry reminder cards for the steps of certain activities, such as riding a bus. Siblings could create the cards together as part of the activity. Other things typical siblings can teach to their brother or sister with ASD include how to go to a restaurant, how to play a game, or how to buy something at a store. It is helpful to learn more about a brother or sister's skills before embarking on projects like these. For example, a sibling can ascertain how much a brother or sister understands about money and math before teaching how to balance a checkbook or pay a restaurant tab.

◆ **Taking on a parental role** for a sibling with ASD is common. This may include living with a sibling when a parent is temporarily unable to or is absent due to divorce or death. Like a parent, a sibling who has taken on such a role can experience a continued sense of worry over a brother or sister, no matter his or her age. When a parent still plays an active role, the typical sibling can set more boundaries. For example, he may offer to attend school meetings regarding goals and behavior plans, but allow the parent to continue to arrange weekend visits away from the group home.

Every sibling will find a different definition of what is a comfortable level of involvement. And this level of comfort is not static; circumstances change. For example, an adult typical sibling may feel she has less to give if she has a new baby, young children, a child in need of special attention, financial challenges, health issues, or marital strain. It is often difficult for siblings to balance the demands of their own lives with those of their family of origin. Nevertheless, it is an important part of maturing and creating a life of one's own. Some siblings find they can play instrumental and even pivotal roles without becoming involved to an overwhelming extent. Staying in close contact with parents to offer support and check in emotionally can have far-reaching positive effects. Such smaller-scale involvements are often overlooked or neglected. In our tendency to think of the more heroic levels of involvement, we often fail to recognize that contact itself has stress-reducing and tie-strengthening qualities.

Even when siblings are the sole familial contact, it may be that a constant, but manageable level of support and involvement can be identified and achieved. For example, many individuals with ASD are comforted by regular contact via mail, phone, or email, when frequent visits are untenable.

◆ Siblings must sometimes **let go of the struggle** to force parents to make future plans for their child with ASD. In the end, siblings cannot make their parents plan or prepare. Sometimes, this means that siblings simply wait to inherit the problem of planning, even though the stress of this burden can be significant. Ideally, siblings could plan along with the parents, who might be more open to planning when a typical sibling becomes part of the process.

One tactic is to write parents a thoughtful, loving letter requesting a joint approach to future planning. Siblings might also participate by, for example, gathering information on financial or estate planning and allowing parents to read the material in their own time (see Appendix C). Siblings have to know whether parents are willing to pursue these avenues with such assistance. Thus, if, in fact, the parents do not want to engage in the process, seeking out contact information may be an exercise in futility. It is important for a typical sibling to recognize that many older people have legitimate concerns about their own futures, including health and finances. As a result, the needs of the parents must be balanced against those of the child with ASD.

◆ Shy or socially anxious typical siblings might put tremendous energy into the role of assisting their sibling with ASD as a way to achieve a "legitimate" **respite from** the **social demands** of their own life without fear of failure.

This is not an altogether bad strategy, as it may bring the typical sibling some joy, and may help cement the bond between siblings. However, it is important for a typical sibling to honestly evaluate whether such involvement constitutes an avoidance of other aspects of life that may ultimately need attention. If social anxiety is a significant issue for the typical sibling, there are many effective ways to build social confidence and to gain support in that area. For example, self-help books might help a sibling learn relaxation techniques that can be used to combat social anxiety. Individual or group therapy focused on social anxiety might also help a sibling (a) identify the most challenging aspects of social situations, (b) desensitize him/herself to the components of those situations, and (c) find comfortable ways to connect with others.

◆ Some typical **siblings put pressure on themselves** to assume responsibility for their brother or sister with ASD. Siblings often feel that by helping parents shoulder this responsibility, they gain increased compassion and maturity and a widened perspective. This is so even if they make sacrifices because of their sibling's disability.

   However, it is important that typical siblings not be unduly burdened. Parents must recognize that their other children (a) are not the parents of the family member with a disability, (b) are entitled to the fun and freedom inherent in childhood, and (c) should not be forced to shoulder responsibility for their sibling with ASD. In fact, coercion in this regard generally breeds resentment rather than compassion. Therefore, it is important that typical children willingly choose their levels of involvement with their brother or sister with ASD.

◆ **Resentment** can weigh heavily when parents abdicate their duties toward their child with ASD, forcing a sibling to step in and fulfill a parenting role. Siblings in this predicament have a dual burden: They must manage the significant emotional impact of the family's failure to cope effectively AND they must mobilize resources for their sibling.

   In such circumstances, professional help is not only beneficial but often necessary, as each of these challenges requires tremendous emotional energy.

◆ In many families, typically developing siblings have varying emotional and financial capacities and **assume roles** toward their sibling with ASD accordingly. Also, it is not uncommon for typical siblings to rotate levels of involvement. Large families usually have more options for finding the level of involvement that is best suited to family resources and personalities.

   A lone typical sibling, of course, does not have this luxury. Nevertheless, typical siblings in this situation may still be able to tailor their niche of involvement by delegating certain responsibilities to others, such as professional staff in their sibling's residence, friends of the family, or concerned relatives. Other sources of support for typical siblings who want help caring for their brother or sister might be special education students from a local university and respite workers from a state or community agency.

◆ It is not uncommon for a sibling to feel **free from any responsibility** for a brother or sister with ASD with comfort and with minimal guilt. Such siblings report that they do not expect to see their brother or sister with ASD except at family gatherings and the like. It is important to realize that the constellations of family patterns of involvement are many and varied. There is no one solution for any individual family or for any particular sibling. It is a challenge for more involved siblings to accept this choice. At times, it can be helpful for the more involved typical sibling to request specific help (i.e., transportation home for a holiday weekend). At other times, it may be more advisable to simply accept the decision of the other siblings to absent themselves from an active role.

Understandable anger and resentment can come along with this acknowledgment of disparity in shouldering the burden. It is often beneficial for the more involved typical siblings to find appropriate outlets for that anger outside of the family; for example, through support groups, therapy, and understanding friends. Some people find it helpful to strive toward acceptance and forgiveness as goals. Also, focusing on the here and now, on building the future, and on accepting the limits of those we love may be very helpful to siblings in this circumstance.

◆ Some siblings aim to make life as productive as possible for their brother or sister – not to find a cure. For example, they may help the sibling learn to balance a checkbook or participate in vocational training. This is part of an effort to **accept the limitations of the disability**, and is part of an acceptance that many siblings demonstrate.

Siblings can demonstrate their love and devotion by focusing on the quality of life that their brother or sister may experience, and on trying to enhance this quality of life in whatever way they can. Some siblings might increase their brother or sister's happiness by sending favorite items, by corresponding regularly, by arranging to spend holidays together, or by taking them on a special outing.

◆ A sibling who feels a strong sense of responsibility might be **angered by a parent's treatment choice** for a brother or sister, especially when it involves institutionalization. Conversely, a sibling might have difficulty coping with parental refusal to find adequate treatment. Placement decisions are complex and never easily navigated. While parents must be supported in making these choices, it is often unclear whether full support or an alternate view is most helpful. Many siblings are torn between their parents and the interests of their sibling in this context.

At such times, it is often beneficial to get counsel from a trusted source who knows the sibling well. A case manager at the group home, a staff psychologist long known to the family, or a former teacher of the individual with ASD may be able to give a more objective view of a situation clouded by emotion. It is also helpful to get a full team report to assess whether there is consensus about the direction to pursue. Often, staff members and professionals who work with the individual with ASD have a clear and coherent sense of his or her needs and may be able to provide more logical and data-based reasons for recommending certain courses of action. Such objectivity can be invaluable, especially in emotionally charged situations.

◆ **A move away** from the area where a sibling with ASD lives may cause typical siblings to feel guilty or tell themselves that the move is only temporary. It is a challenge for a typical sibling to feel entitled to create an independent life, particularly if it involves geographical distance. Many siblings feel a sense of obligation that pervades their choices in a long-term sense.

There is no simple answer. As with much of life, it becomes a question of balance. Siblings are not choosing their own life over supporting their family of origin; they are simply living their lives. Siblings must come to understand that geographical distance does not preclude meaningful engagement and involvement, just as geographical closeness does not ensure active participation in the life of the sibling or in the larger family context.

Comfort with one's decision is of central importance. Siblings must determine what they can live with and what they cannot, and how they can be involved and how they cannot. If a decision to move is coupled with a clear articulation of the ways they plan to remain involved, the effects of the move are usually less dramatic.

◆ Siblings may feel a larger sense of **responsibility to all people with ASD** as a result of their relationship with their brother or sister. This may manifest itself in various ways, especially in career choices.

Many siblings feel a sense of mission about helping individuals with ASD and their families. They often want to have an impact on individuals with ASD on a broader scale. At other times, siblings develop a more global people orientation. They may focus on enhancing the lives of others in need and may give of themselves in many personal and professional activities.

Chapter 4

The Emotional Consequences: Experiencing ASD's Impact Personally

aving a sibling with ASD has wide-reaching emotional consequences. The emotions are strong, and they are variable. The intensity of their emotions sometimes took our interviewees by surprise, both while growing up and in adulthood.

Handling the emotional impact of having a sibling with ASD is a daunting task. And siblings often navigate these rough and unfamiliar waters alone, afraid to burden their parents with their needs. Coming to terms with the emotional impact and relating their experiences to others gave our interviewees perspective, helped them feel less alone in the universe, and allowed them to move on to accepting the reality of their sibling's disability.

One of the most significant ways typical siblings are affected by ASD is in the realm of personal relationships. Some siblings we interviewed mentioned a pattern of dating people who had serious challenges of their own. These included people with substance abuse problems, mental health issues, physical challenges, or difficult personality traits.

In this section, we will take a look at the broad range of emotions typical siblings experience when they have a brother or sister with ASD. We will also find out how some siblings approach and handle their personal relationships in light of these emotions.

Emotions

Anger: A Powerful Emotion

Anger is one of the deepest and most intense emotions that we experience as humans. It is an emotion that does not disappear and sometimes leads to actions that we come to regret or feel ashamed of.

Anger is a significant issue for families with individuals with disabilities. Siblings can experience anger at many different developmental stages. As children, typical siblings may feel neglected when so much energy goes to the family member with ASD. Thus, typical siblings may be angry at parents who give more time and attention to the sibling with ASD. They may also feel angry at the impact ASD has on the family, in terms of missed social opportunities or continual accommodations to the presence of ASD in the family. Moreover, a sibling may be directly angry at a brother or sister with ASD for being the center of attention and for draining family resources.

Typical siblings may feel angry, in general, at having to live with ASD when so many other people do not. This is especially true in adolescence, when it is most important to fit in, to have a conventional life. Feelings of anger often continue in adulthood, although the themes change. For example, now anger at parents may reflect the frustration of trying to plan for the future while parents remain in denial about the inevitability of the changes that come with time. And some adults report waves of anger, resentment, or regret over simply having a life that is more complex and sadder than that of most families.

An interesting aspect of the sibling experience in this regard is that many siblings do not express their feelings of anger. Many do not even become well aware of their anger until much later in life. This is probably the result of powerful, although subtle, messages that the expression of such anger would be a further burden to an already overburdened family. The result is an isolation and loneliness that prevents family members from accessing support from each other.

Most of the siblings we talked to did not report feeling angry at the moment, but some had vivid memories of angry times.

Anna Reed: I remember being a little kid and being really angry at his behavior. I locked myself in my room and I remember saying to myself, "He's retarded, he's retarded!" I thought I was being very horrible to say that – but it made me feel better to know that there was a reason for his behavior.

Jessica Golden: I'm not angry or anything. I think my mom did the best she could. Could I have done it better? No way! I would have done worse. I don't know how she did it, to be honest with you. I really respect her.

Lynne Stern Feiges: I have had to come to terms this year with the anger I feel about Rich's situation. Angry doesn't begin to describe how I felt watching my brother slowly dying in an institution, or seeing my parents age about 20 years in just a few months. Now that Rich is in a stable environment again, I am trying to let go of my anger about what he experienced. It's hard, though. I get so enraged when I think about my brother rotting away in that institution. What was his crime, being born with a disability? It's just outrageous.

Sarah Cooper: Rick was about 7, and we were on the beach when some kid wanted to play with him. He asked my mother whether Rick was deaf, and I remember thinking, "My God, he's not deaf, just autistic! He can hear!"

Always in Crisis

One of the hardest parts of living with a person with ASD is the constant sense that the family is walking on eggshells. For some of the interviewees, this sense of impending doom was a constant source of tension. Living with such tension has consequences. It is difficult for families to "let loose" under such circumstances. While other families are spontaneously deciding to catch fireflies or do a monkey dance, a family with a child with ASD might be trying to just keep things predictable, to not "rock the boat," to avoid provoking a behavioral incident. While this may be necessary to maintain stability, it can result in lost spontaneity and, to some extent, joy.

Anna Reed: I remember going through some period where I was upset a lot. I don't know what about. But there was always such an intense level of crisis going on. Joseph was the crisis always – everything else paled.

Lynne Stern Feiges: We are the best crisis managers on the planet in my family. My mother, for example, she can't even operate the VCR, but handling a giant health, financial, or emotional crisis, no problem! My parents are the first I call when there's trouble. I know that they will instantly start trying to solve whatever the problem is in any way they can. I always feel I can count on them to come up with a few good ideas, at the very least. This is the result, of course, of always waiting for the other shoe to drop regarding Rich's behavior or placement, or both. I feel sad about this sometimes. I appreciate what living under siege has done for all of us, but I would have chosen to live without that, given the choice.

Frustration

Frustration is a natural emotion for siblings of individuals with ASD. There is frustration with the family situation, when the family cannot do what other families do. There is frustration with the ASD behaviors themselves. (Why does he still scream like that?) There may be frustration with the slow progress or lack of progress in a certain area, such as when the speech of the sibling with a disability remains difficult to comprehend or when he or she continues to need assistance getting dressed. And sometimes there is frustration with the permanence of ASD, with the fact that even when progress is being made, the disorder stays.

Anna Reed: He has his license and drives once a week to the supermarket with my mother at 3 p.m. on Sunday. It drives me crazy because it's such a ritualistic thing!

Sam Cohen: I get very frustrated at the lack of being able to communicate with him. I'll ask him a direct, simple question and I can't get a direct, simple answer. If my wife asks him, he'll talk. He'll respond clearer and with more affect.

Leslie Cohen: I wish I had more patience to deal with him and try and show him things. I don't know whether it means anything to him, but I want him to feel like he's contributing. I'd like for him to be as happy as he can be. Have what he wants.

Julie Shore: I used to be in a therapy group at school. The counselor always drove me nuts because she made me feel worse. I'll talk about it, I just don't like talking about it over and over and over. It's like obsessive talking!

Michael Stern: I have always felt frustrated over not being able to communicate with Rich. Who wouldn't be? As I've gotten older, I've been less so. There are still times now that I get frustrated.

Embarrassment

Embarrassment was a common and memorable emotional experience for the siblings we spoke with. Many could recall situations of acute embarrassment with a freshness that defied the passage of time. Embarrassment is a raw and painful emotion.

While many siblings expressed embarrassment while growing up, some also spoke of it in their adult lives. Many told us honestly that they still feel embarrassed by their sibling's behavior, even when they wish they did not.

It is especially difficult to be around people who don't understand and people who don't accept a person with ASD. And as much as we might know that it reflects the narrow-mindedness or limits of the person who doesn't understand, it still hurts when our brother or sister is looked at or treated with disdain, ridicule, or cruelty.

Anna Reed: We [my other siblings and I] used to invite him to go along with us to places as a kid, and we knew he wouldn't go. But I would hope that he wouldn't go! We'd always invite him but hope that he wouldn't because he was so embarrassing. I'm embarrassed of him now. A little less so, now that I think of him as disabled.

I feel like I could always do more. I could take him out and teach him better social skills. And yet, I don't want to. It's so unpleasant for me, embarrassing. And the obligation annoys me. Sometimes I have so much more patience for my clients than for my family.

Jeremy Plant: Eli is real open. When others come over, he'll sit down and have a whole conversation. He'll go up to people in stores, too. In Wal-Mart once — I had been babysitting and forgot to give him his meds — he put up a big stink, started yelling and screaming. I didn't really get embarrassed by it, I figured that people could say what they want about him. Who cares! But in my freshman year, at one of my sporting events, my mom had him in the stands (my dad has a lot more control over him than my mom), and Eli was yelling and screaming. At the time, it was embarrassing. I'm like, "Oh my god, mom, get him out of here." Now, I would say, well, what can I do about it? Eli is not as bad as a lot of people make him out to be.

Becky Lott: When I was younger, I was embarrassed. I didn't want my friends to know I had an autistic brother. Even though he doesn't look autistic, people would try to talk with him and he wouldn't talk back. I got embarrassed by that. Now it doesn't bother me. I saw that there were more people out there like Gordon. Growing up, I got better with it. It all sort of evolved.

Jessica Golden: I was embarrassed of him. He hated wearing clothes, so he'd take them off and run around the neighborhood. I was horrified. When he was mainstreamed, my mom sat me down and told me he was coming to my school. I remember not being happy with him in my school.

Will was teased so bad. During recess, one of the kids found poison from the janitor's cleaning stuff and they poured it down his back. He suffered second- and third-degree burns and was medivaced to a hospital. So, not only did I have this strange brother, but now he had burns all over his back. I tried to stick up for him. I hit a few kids. My younger brother and I always had to defend Will. When this happened, my first thought was, if I had been there, this wouldn't have happened. I always looked out for him in recess because we had it at the same time. They were so mean to him!

Will wanted so bad to fit in. He told me that. He tried everything just to belong. When he was in 7th grade, he ran for student body president – the biggest geek there was. I remember telling my mother that I could not believe he was doing it. I said he was ruining my life! Of course, he lost. But he always had the balls to do that. He almost tried too hard. I'd tell him to lie low because I didn't want him to make a spectacle of himself. It probably wasn't the most supportive thing, but being a teenager, I don't know what else a teenager would say to her brother.

In grade school and junior high, Will didn't know when to be quiet or what to say. My grandmother had a party, and he said really loud, "Why doesn't that woman shave her mustache!" He's so impulsive. Even after the autism "passed," there was still cognition stuff and he was still needy. The chronic nature didn't go away.

Sarah Cooper: I've never been embarrassed of Rick until about a year ago. I was with my in-laws, who are very worldly. I brought them over and they were very on edge. Rick was there. It frustrated me that they were so quiet about it. They don't talk around Rick, they wait for him to leave. They don't know what to do. We were all in the kitchen, and all of a sudden Rick put both of his hands down his pants and started scratching and scratching. I didn't know what to do! I couldn't get him to stop. We were all grabbing a hand, and my mother-in-law asked, "Where did he learn that?" I'm like, "What do you think, I sent him to the masturbation school?" Turns out he had a rash. I was embarrassed because they were embarrassed.

Dana Peters: It was harder when he became an adult and he'd act up. Here he is this larger person, and it was no longer acceptable.

Bethany Powers: I tried to ignore her as much as possible. I remember I was hideously shamed and embarrassed by her. I didn't want to invite friends over to the house and say that I had this sister. I would only say that she was emotionally disturbed.

75

A pivotal moment in my life was in 7th grade in English class, where you'd be called on to get in front of the class and talk about yourself. I just said I had two sisters – nothing about Emma. Then another girl got up and said her sister was retarded. Nobody laughed at her or made fun of her. She was a popular girl and a nice girl, and I felt like a worm. I took a little vow that day that I wasn't going to conceal my sister any more. I would talk about her if it came up – and I did it from that day on. But this didn't change how I felt inside. I still felt very much ashamed of her, and the anxiety was still very much there well into my 20s.

At 16, a friend of mine was going to be in town and was looking for a place to crash one night. Emma was home for the summer. I was really anxious. I didn't want him to see her! I wondered what he would think, and this wasn't even a guy I liked particularly at all!

As an adult I've come to believe that the vast majority of people are only thinking nice things. I truly believe that, and also that nearly everyone has something in their life that they can connect to emotionally and put themselves in your place. I really believe that, but sometimes these old things kick in anyway. Or sometimes my sister will do something I find particularly embarrassing. Restaurants are pretty much OK now, but if she eats something she doesn't like (such as onions), she'll scream and spit out the food. That can be very embarrassing. I feel I have become better about it – that this is 90 percent my problem. I've always been especially hard on myself.

I remember going out to lunch with her and nearly dying of humiliation when she made a scene at the restaurant. The waitress took me aside and said, "There, there, it's fine." Which was even more humiliating!

Lynne Stern Feiges: We used to take Rich everywhere when he was a kid. It wasn't until much later that we would worry about unpredictable behavioral outbursts in public. One time, we were at a kosher butcher shop in town. My mom used to stock up on meat all at once. So, there we were, my mom, Rich, and I (I guess I was in middle school). The cart was full of meat, must have been several hundred dollars' worth, and we were waiting in line to pay. Rich became agitated and started tapping the cart and yelling at my mom. It was obvious he was disabled, but the owner of the shop started yelling at him and told my mom to essentially get him out of there.

I was stunned someone could be so unsympathetic. Then my mom pushed the cart into the middle of the isle and told the owner where he could stick his meat. We walked out with our heads held high. I wasn't embarrassed at all, I was so proud of my mother. It was like, "Yeah!!"

I'm not embarrassed of Rich in the sense that his autism shames me. When he was institutionalized, though, I just found it ironic and unbelievable that a member of my family would end up at a place like that. I mean, my parents always did 300 percent for us and always sought to protect us from things. And then that happened. It was such a rude awakening.

Leslie Cohen: We tried to include him in stuff. The only problem I had was when we swam and he couldn't understand that they had to have a pool check. He would have a tantrum and we'd have to physically take him out. Everyone would be looking at us. It was kind of traumatizing. But I'd react toward the other people like, "You got a problem?" not toward Marc.

I'm not embarrassed now. I try to get him to behave in an acceptable manner. I want him to know he needs to follow some standards when he's out.

Julie Shore: I don't like going anywhere with my parents or brother. Between my parents' conversations and Robby's babbling, I just don't like it!

Maryann Hall: Kids stare at her when they come over like she's an alien or something because they've never seen anything like it. I feel embarrassed because I don't want a sister who is stared at, and it makes me feel different from everybody else.

It makes me feel good to be around other families [with kids with disabilities] because when it's just me and my family, it feels like I am the only one.

Lance Strong: It can be embarrassing in public places, and he starts making weird noises. He used to ride the bus to school, make noises, and get the whole bus going. I was on the bus, too. I just sort of sat there. I sometimes don't know why he just can't stop. All he really has to do is shut his mouth. It's not so hard to do, but I guess it's difficult for him.

Michael Stern: I was the only one in the family growing up that felt ashamed of Rich. I felt weak compared to my other family members.

Perfectionism

One of the occasional consequences in a family with a child with ASD is that typically developing children become very high-striving or perfection-istic. This may be because they are trying to make up for the fact that their brother or sister with ASD will not be able to achieve in more nor-mative ways. Nevertheless, some siblings who become very successful experience it in a bittersweet way. While there is joy in their accomplish-ments, there is also a sadness in the recognition of the contrast between their fate and the fate of their brother or sister with ASD.

Sometimes the desire for perfection among typical siblings is about wanting to ensure that they do not add to their parents' burden. So, many of these children focus on being self-sufficient, on being the quiet, competent one, on being the one no one "needs to worry about." In the process, they sometimes create a situation in which parental atten-tion feels inadequate. In addition, a strong perfectionistic tendency may alienate other important people in the sibling's life. In childhood, for example, typical peers may find it annoying or boring. Certainly, many typically developing youngsters do not relate to perfectionism, which may make social connections more tenuous or superficial. In adulthood, spouses and friends may tire of perfectionism, and it may create tension or a fear of judgment. Furthermore, a continued tendency to "cope perfectly" often leaves the typical sibling alone in his or her stress. We benefit most from support when we ask for it, when we attempt to access it, and when we are open to receiving it.

Anna Reed: I felt that I had to do everything perfectly because if I didn't, maybe that meant I was disabled.

Bethany Powers: I took the "perfect" route. I felt that my parents had enough troubles in their life and that, therefore, I couldn't give them any trouble. I certainly didn't get the attention that I wanted. I learned to read at a young age and tried to read aloud to my parents to show them. I remember my mother saying to my father, "Bethany's alright, she's fine on her own." So this bid for attention by reading aloud had the opposite effect. I took this to heart and tried repeatedly to demonstrate how I didn't need, didn't need, didn't need. This was how I got love and approval. Bethany didn't need anything.

Michael Stern: I felt a constant need for recognition both in and out of my family circle. I excelled at various things, as well as undertaking new things that separated me from my peers. I was argumentative and irreverent; difficult at times. Always the faithful son but a royal pain in the ass.

Julie Shore: I don't try to be the "good child" because I don't think it's fair that he gets all the attention. He knows what he's doing. He's being manipulative and getting exactly what he wants because he realizes he has an excuse. I'm not gonna be the kid who sits there and won't say anything and doesn't deal with my problems because of him!

Lynne Stern Feiges: The desire not to rock the boat and add to my parents' burden is deeply ingrained in me. When I got married, I felt huge guilt about taking money from them for this large wedding we were planning. I wanted a big party, but I felt I was being frivolous taking money away from my younger brothers with disabilities, who would surely need those resources for more important things. We ended up having a big, fat, gorgeous wedding. And, looking back, I think it was one of the happiest days in our family's history. Something I initially perceived as burdensome for them was nothing but positive and joyous.

Worry

Part of being a sibling of a person with ASD is considering what the future will hold for everybody – siblings, with and without a disability – and the family. The more time that passes, the more siblings become aware of the need for future planning.

Jeremy Plant: I think, what's gonna happen when he gets to middle school. Are people going to accept him? It's a real sensitive time and everyone's trying to fit in. A lot of people make fun of special ed kids there.

Sarah Cooper: I worry about Rick's future daily. I worry that the group home is going to end and he's going to be released. It's something I think about all the time. I fear he'll have to go to an institution. I mean, he won't. I'll quit my job and stay home if I have to. But I worry about his future all the time. His seizures are horrific. I'm afraid if he becomes too hard to handle, he'll get thrown out.

Lynne Stern Feiges: Right after Rich was placed in his new program, the state froze all funding for placements such as this. But for the grace of God go I ... He would have been stuck in that godforsaken institution, and you can only imagine the rest. I sometimes get to thinking that the floor will fall out from under us again, and this instills absolute terror in me. I know that this may be a possibility; you never know how things will work out. But if I give in to the fear and worry, it's crippling. I have to consciously force myself not to think about all that.

Jessica Golden: I was in support groups as a teenager. I was talking to other siblings about how we felt. And [because of Will's higher functioning] the other siblings would say to me, "Well, your brother's gonna be OK, and you're not gonna have to take care of him or put him in a group home." That struck me that I am really lucky. I meet siblings who are dealing with things I'll never have to deal with. He still impacted my life, though, even though I'll never have to deal with what happens when my mom dies.

Pain over Being a Parent and Sibling

A profound and unique pain was expressed by our interviewee whose roles in life included being both a sister of a person with ASD and a mother of a child with ASD. The fear of reliving the past is paralyzing and almost unbearable.

Olivia Hanover: The day we went to take Joshua to a specialist in New York, he was the worst he could have been. It was heart-wrenching. My mother went with me, and my brother arranged for a car to take us into the city. I will tell you, the whole way back I was silent. It was too much for me to absorb, and I started thinking all over, "Oh no, I'm going to relive the hell I knew as a child."

Unfairness/Regret

Siblings we spoke to also expressed sadness at the unfairness of it all. It is inherently unfair that some of us are born with disabilities that will affect everything about our lives. Living with that reality makes siblings acutely aware of the unfairness of life. They feel pangs of sorrow when they realize that their brother or sister with ASD will miss certain experiences and particular milestones.

At the same time, there is often a personal regret, a sense of loss of what they could have had with a sibling without disabilities. There is a longing that does not go away, a wondering that persists.

Ashley Williams: Every day I feel upset about how incredibly unfair it is to Todd and about how I don't get to have a "normal" sibling like some of my friends do. Yet, I interact with him the way I know how, and most of the time we can communicate and I'm at least happy we're able to do that.

Dana Peters: I think that I wish he could do things for himself, and not so much for [the benefit of] our interaction. I remember saying to my sister, "Wow, he'd be driving now." What was hard for me growing up was that my friends would have brothers the same age. He actually has grown up, but he's always just been my little brother.

Jordan Cohen: I remember going to the rabbi and asking, "Why would God do this?" He said something like, "The bad happens so you can appreciate the good." I felt this was totally insufficient.

Julie Shore: I just look at friends who have humongous families and think if only I had just one normal sibling.

Lance Strong: The bad side of having a normal sibling would be that he'd bug you and do all the little-brother stuff that Michael didn't really do. But I'd much rather have a normal sibling.

I feel different in a good way and a bad way. I get to experience and know a person like Michael. To understand people who are different. But I don't have a normal brother and a lot of my friends have normal brothers and sisters that they do things with.

Sadness

The siblings we spoke to expressed sadness most of all. This sadness is pervasive – it extends to parents, to the individual with ASD, and to the siblings themselves. Many typical siblings feel a special sadness for their parents. They feel their pain acutely. There is a sense of loss; loss of the normal, loss of the ordinary. And while acceptance of difference was compelling and common, sadness was a theme throughout our interviews.

Dana Peters: In terms of the big picture, I think sadness sort of captures it. I shift a lot of energy to myself, thinking that if I'm stronger, I can help. I definitely go through days when I cry about it, over how we're going to do this. But it comes and it goes. I think every family's got it's "stuff," and this is our stuff.

Lynne Stern Feiges: I was, and still am, very keyed into my mother's pain about Rich. When I was about 7, I remember spying on her while she sobbed in the kitchen. Apparently, she had been told Rich needed to be institutionalized. She was just wailing. This vision has never left me; it's made an indelible stamp. A child's pain is also a parent's. I think it works the other way as well. Last summer, when Rich was sent to a state institution (the day we all feared had finally arrived), I was giving my daughter a bath, and I just broke down thinking about it all. I tried to turn my head so that she wouldn't see me upset, but she knew anyway. She just patted my arm and said, "It's OK mommy, it's OK." I'm grateful to have such a compassionate child, but I feel guilty about letting her see my emotional pain. In the final analysis, though, pain is part of life, and she will be a better person if she understands this.

The very worst part of all of this, for me, is watching my parents suffer. When things were stable with Rich, there was still a low-grade sense of worry, but life pretty much went on. Not so any more. And now that I'm a parent, I truly understand the misery they must feel. There's nothing worse, really, than having something wrong with your kid.

Guilt

The reality of growing up and moving on is often difficult, and guilt is a common consequence. Of course, people are entitled to forge ahead, to create a life. Every adolescent and young adult feels entitled to craft a life for themselves. But the process of separating from family is much more complex when there is a member with ASD. That is, while there is a push to move on, even to move from the family, at the same time there is a pull to stay, to help, to always be there, to support the parents, to take up the cause of caring for the sibling.

Most siblings find a middle ground. They spend their early adulthoods defining the roles they feel comfortable with and creating a life apart from their families of origin to varying extents. But often, guilt is a consequence of these compromises and choices. It is impossible not to feel some guilt as they hear the continued struggles that characterize their sibling's life and as they continue to hear their parents tell tales of woe and worry about their brother or sister.

Jamie Cohen: I feel, because I'm here in California, that I don't see him enough. I'm his guardian, but I don't see him more than a few times a year. We talk to him every week, and I feel good about that. But I don't know him as well as I used to. I feel guilty I'm on the other coast. I should be taking care of him.

Sam Cohen: There was a lot of guilt; it was strange. For years and years, I was guilty that I didn't do as much for Marc as everyone else did. Everyone else wasn't out of the house, living somewhere else, married young with a new family. No one else had those situations going on.

My sibs had always been more involved with him up until the last few years. My brother Jordan and sisters have always been resentful. I would explain that I had a stressful career and family, and I felt guilty about it! (It's hardwired!) Now, part of me feels like it's my time to take care of him. I'm better able to now, without a doubt: I'm in a nice stable marriage, made it through a downsizing at work.

I still find myself getting very impatient with him, which does not make me feel good. I feel guilty about the fact that being in public with him embarrasses me more than I think it should. For instance, I'll go into a restaurant with him and I'll see the waitress' reaction to him and I'll feel embarrassed. And then I feel bad about that.

Michael Stern: I have a very distant relationship with Rich. He's been out of my life for so long that there is little emotional investment in our relationship. However, I do worry about his well-being and I want to make sure he is properly cared for.

Acceptance

Many of the siblings we spoke to eloquently expressed a profound and genuine acceptance of their brother or sister with ASD. While they had no choice in the matter, they have made peace with their reality. They expressed love for and connection with their siblings with ASD. They expressed feeling that their brother or sister with ASD was a "part of their own," a person who belonged to and with them. They also expressed hope for their futures

Jeremy Plant: Now I realize, hey, he's my only brother and I have to accept the fact that he's not the typical brother. You know, though, we still have our fun. I don't look at him any differently for being that way. When my parents divorced, I finally accepted this. At first, I thought, when my dad moved out, that maybe he was giving up. But I've realized in the past couple of years that that wasn't the case. Because now my dad has him more than my mom does. I realize that my dad cares about him a lot.

Sarah Cooper: I never felt any kind of regret. I never dwelled on the fact that I couldn't talk to my brother about field hockey or something. I never thought hard about "what if?" There really was no time. If I thought like that, it would be destructive. I accept him for what he is because I know he gives me the best that he can. He's come a long way. This was a kid who wasn't supposed to talk or communicate. He also has seizures almost daily, so the fact that he wakes up in the morning and wants cereal is something to cherish.

For someone who will never be normal in life, I have a lot of respect for him. He goes through this knock-down, drag-down seizure every night and, you know, he's getting through the day. How many people could go through that night after night!

Susan Peters: I never got frustrated over our interaction. I really accepted it. But, I mean, I wonder what it would be like to have a brother to interact normally with.

Bethany Powers: Over time I have come to find ways in which she is supportive to me. I have this irrational fear that if everything's not perfect in Emma's world, terrible things will happen. I think her world would be richer if she had more people in her life. I want to help make that happen.

Jamie Cohen: To this day, I'm still frustrated with what [ASD] is and how you help someone who is blessed with it. I always want to educate myself more about it.

Sam Cohen: I'm the one who lives near Marc now. He has always been intimidated by me, doesn't talk to me. He talks to my wife nonstop, though. We have him over once a week. It doesn't hurt me that he doesn't talk to me. My brother Jordan's theory is that this is the way he reacts to males versus females.

My attitude is that he's never going to be any better, stronger, or more communicative than he is now. I more or less accept that.

If someone ever asks about my family, I tell them the truth. I include Marc. But it's equal to everything else emotionally. He is not more compelling than my relationship with my other siblings. I never would have viewed myself as being cold, but others have accused me of it.

Personal Relationships

Many typical siblings reported that they felt compelled to "fix" and/or caretake their partners and friends. Also, some siblings felt tremendous empathy for those who might be seen as difficult, unusual, or outcasts. Such openness to diversity and capacity for compassion are wonderful traits; however, they sometimes led our interviewees into relationships they saw as unhealthy in retrospect.

Anna Reed: I definitely dated and still date people I need to fix. I lock into somebody and I think, if I work hard enough, they can be fixed. Or I stay away because I'm sick of being the caretaker! My first significant relationship was when I lived with this man who was a dependent personality type – someone who needed a mommy. Over the past three years, off and on, I've dated a substance abuser. And I'm so not that way. When I see him, he doesn't use, so I get to have this major denial ... like gee, there's a disabled person here, let's acknowledge it ... Gee, he's a substance abuser, but not when he's with me ... and he needs all this help and has personality stuff from the way he was treated ... his mom was a teenage mom and my heart goes out to him ... If I could just wait long enough and do just the right things, he'll become the perfect mate for me ...

There's a lot of that feeling of being lovable when I'm giving. This man I was seeing was a social worker but also a masseuse. I always wished he would offer to give me a massage but it's his job and he never did. One day he gave me a back massage, which is what I had wanted, and I started crying. It was so hard just to take. It is a really vulnerable position not to be on that giving end and still be OK.

Jessica Golden: I had this other guy I dated for a long time who was very emotionally needy and did a lot of stupid things. I was always there to pick up the pieces. He even tried to commit suicide and, of course, "I saved him." (I'm not sure why now!) My husband always jokes when we talk about people I dated that I chose every person with a problem!

I dated this one guy, who my mother called her fourth kid. He's still a part of our family. He really took care of Jeremy. When I met him, I knew there was something about him. I came right out and said, "So, are you learning disabled?" He was like, "How'd you know?" At 17, I just knew. We went out for a while. I pushed him to college.

Susan Peters: I find myself drawn to people who are nurturing and very caring and in need of more attention. I dated someone who was blind. Looking back, I wonder if I needed to have someone need me for something or depend on me more.

Leslie Cohen: The person I've been involved with on and off for years has all sorts of dependency problems. He's always saying, "You're not my mother." My sister's the same way. We are overly maternal, and I think people get real tired of it.

Michael Stern: I probably dated a few girls with mental illness, but they disguised it well. I am drawn to people who are unusual or outcasts.

Sarah Cooper: I never dated someone with mental illness, but I'm definitely the caretaker in my marriage – the need to please kind of thing. I'm sure it has a lot to do with Rick. In terms of friendships, growing up I was very intense. I was always looking for lifelong friends, and I think that it scared a lot of people off. I was always very serious with my friendships, and it backfired. When, as teenagers, others just wanted to have fun, I was always very into "the relationship." Maybe I wanted someone to mother me like I mothered Rick. I wanted a closer kinship. But it's strange because I never felt like I needed a brother or sister. I had trouble keeping friends because I was so serious.

Ashley Williams: I am usually the caretaker in personal relationships. Whenever I am with my friends, I tend to be the one talking about responsibility and the one that's always there to listen and help with my friends' problems. I'll admit at times, I do hate being that way and want to be more carefree. Yet, I realize I can't change the way I am, so I just accept it.

Jamie Cohen: My husband is younger than I am. A lot of times, I feel in certain situations, I might do things the same way I might do it with Marc.

Connecting and Integrating with Others

Occasionally, typical siblings are so affected by their family experience that they become reluctant to pursue a romantic relationship or marriage. While some might feel comfortable with this decision, others might become filled with regret and wonder what might have been. Because siblings often hold their brother or sister with ASD in a very protected place within their hearts, it is very important to them that their sibling with ASD is accepted by those they love. Some siblings report that opening their sibling with ASD to others was an act of immense trust and vulnerability.

Bethany Powers: There have been very few romantic relationships. I think I looked at my parents' marriage and the tremendous strain my sister had been on them. I didn't like their marriage. I thought marriage sucks for women and that men were big leaches.

Dana Peters: If you knew about Chris, it meant you were very close to me. How much a person knows about my brother is indicative of how close I am to them. I mean, you don't just go around talking about that. How people respond to the issue – how much attention or empathy they give it – is how I gauge that person. In terms of the questions they ask me, that tells me a lot about their personality. Many times it's been a turn-off!

Jordan Cohen: I didn't introduce any women to Marc unless there was a strong possibility of the relationship going anywhere.

Susan Peters: I definitely make it known to whomever I'm with that it's something that will be a big part of my life in the future. I have a hard time thinking of him in a group home, so I definitely see him living with me and my family. I worry that it might cause problems. It just depends on when this happens.

Julie Shore: I have one friend who has a brother with Asperger's, so she understands a lot, and she's one of my best friends. Her brother is not like Robby too much, but he sits around singing show tunes!

Moving on with one's life entails a certain amount of distancing from what one has known and experienced. For example, entering a family by marriage that has not lived with ASD is, in some ways, like entering foreign territory. Typical siblings usually learn to exist in the two different worlds, but it is often a very rattling and eye-opening experience. While the typical sibling has always known that other families do not have the same kinds of struggles as they did, it is entirely different to (partly) become one of those families.

Lynne Stern Feiges: Getting engaged was pretty traumatic for me. In addition to the typical stress of planning a wedding and melding two families, I was facing a larger internal struggle about breaking away. All these good "wedding" things were happening to me – parties, gifts – I felt more than a little guilty about it all. It seemed frivolous compared to my nuclear family's struggles. Once my mom came to Milwaukee to attend an engagement party, and we were driving in the car along with one of my mother-in-law's friends, who was in the back seat with my mother. Everyone was talking at once. My mom was telling the friend about our family and how my two younger siblings had disabilities, and at the same time, my mother-in-law was telling us about her community, including where she shopped and worked and whatnot. The contrast was overwhelming for me, and I knew then that I had to learn to straddle both worlds – that I was entering a family that had not been forced to deal with chronic stress and that this was another way of life.

Having Your Own Family

Fear of having a child with ASD is an unshared and acute burden experienced by many typical siblings as a logical extension of the experience of growing up in a family with a member with a disability. The fear is fueled by genetic research, which indicates a higher level of risk for these siblings compared to the general population. Even if the risk is still small (statistically speaking), there is nothing small about the emotional risk of having a child with a disability. It is a gut-wrenching and deeply felt fear. While people who grew up without this experience can be naïve about its impact, such a stance is not possible for typical siblings of people with ASD. Nevertheless, some siblings are able to put their fears into perspective – or even aside – and continue forward with their personal dreams of a family.

Anna Reed: As far as having children myself, it would be my nightmare to have a disabled child. I would almost forego having kids than take that risk.

Becky Lott: Now that I'm getting older, because I do want to have kids, I am worrying about it a little bit. If I'll have an autistic child or not ... and how would I deal with that. Like my parents have? Would I freak out and try to give the baby up? I don't know.

Jessica Golden: The issue of having a child with special needs comes up all the time. It's absolutely horrible. I'm scared to death to have children. Absolutely, and it's more on my end. My husband thinks I'm paranoid because I work with it all day long. If I have a handicapped kid, I'll die. I don't even know how I would function. I'm embarrassed to say this. There are a lot of learning disabled people in my family. Funky stuff. Several cousins have disabilities. I know it's there, and it's scary. I feel like I know I'm going to have a kid and automatically they're going to have something. When I have a kid, I'm telling you, I'm going to be freaked out until that kid is 2 or 3. I'm going to be a complete nut case. My husband thinks I'm going to drive him insane!

Ashley Williams: I am afraid of having children. The statistic supposedly is that siblings of children with autism have a 50 percent greater chance than others of having a child with autism. I fear the day where I have to sit down and decide if I want to try and have a child and deal with the possibility of the child having autism. I don't think it would be fair for me to bring a child into this world with him having autism just so I can satisfy my own selfish reasons of wanting to have a child.

Dana Peters: If this were to happen to me [having an autistic child], I hope I'm as strong as my parents. As I'm getting older, I'm thinking how lucky Chris was for my parents.

Sam Cohen: In my second marriage, my wife was 36 when my daughter was born. I always related the fact that my mother was 44 when Marc was born to the autism. Had she been younger … it wouldn't have happened. It was an emotional thing that I don't still believe.

Michael Stern: I have two beautiful healthy kids, but there were moments of anxiety during both pregnancies.

Sarah Cooper: My husband has schizophrenia and manic depression on his side of the family, and I think he was more worried about that [than the autism]. I don't necessarily think autism's genetic, so I didn't have any fears when I was pregnant. I'd like to think I'm intuitive and would have felt something if there were a problem. After I had my daughter, my mother confessed that she was very worried and concerned and scared for me.

When my daughter was 2 weeks old, she was really attracted to the light, which most babies are. My husband and I looked at each other like, Oh no! Another Rick! But we just laughed it off.

Jordan Cohen: Honestly, the thought of being afraid to have children has never occurred to me. Any relationship I've ever been in, no one has ever asked that question. It is a statistical anomaly. It is infinitesimally remote.

Jamie Cohen: My husband has always been very sensitive about Marc, which was real important to me. He said, regarding kids, "Whatever you get is who you love."

Situations and Solutions

◆ Many siblings of individuals with ASD do not have a suffi-
cient understanding of or the **ability to express** their
unique emotional experiences. Part of this is developmental. We tend to become much more articulate and aware
of our emotions as we age. Part of this is also the unique-
ness of the circumstance; it is hard to express one's feelings
when they seem so discrepant from the experiences and
feelings of others, in particular of peers.

Some siblings reach out within their families, and find
solace and comprehension in parents and fellow siblings.
Others reach out by joining a support group or getting
information through books, the Internet, and similar
resources (see listings in Appendix C).

◆ **Anger** is an ever-present emotion – and one that a typical sibling must learn to cope with. Typical siblings feel
angry over many things, including their sense of power-
lessness over their brother or sister's ASD, or their parents' methods of dealing with (or not dealing with) the
situation. One of the hardest things about anger is learning to identify it accurately. Being able to pinpoint the
source of anger is immensely helpful in comprehending
and managing it. It prevents the misattribution of anger
and (hopefully) the misdirection of anger at, for example,
colleagues or members of the public.

Some signs that anger may be an unresolved issue
include obvious ones such as irritability or explosiveness
(even about unrelated issues) and less obvious ones such as
feelings of helplessness or hopelessness. Since many negative health effects are associated with an angry disposition, it
is in a sibling's best interests to address anger in a proactive
manner. Getting through and past anger frees one up to
focus on the other aspects of life that may otherwise be
neglected. That may include fostering a connection with a

sibling with ASD, being able to bond with parents on other matters, and even building an independent life.

Managing anger is a formidable challenge. However, it is generally well worth the effort as reducing anger can be emancipating. Anger has a way of constricting us, of narrowing our focus, and of diminishing our capacity for happiness. The best reason to commit to reducing anger is to increase one's personal happiness as more emotional energy will be available for positivity and joy. Some people find it helpful to identify sources of anger in order to truly understand the content of the emotion. In and of itself, the process of coming to terms with the reasons for anger sometimes helps us feel less intensely angry.

At times, it may also be helpful to share one's angry feelings with appropriate parties. Some siblings have confronted non-involved siblings, for example. While this can be helpful, especially if it is tied to a specific request for change, it can also result in increased tension and heartache. Thus, it may be more beneficial to express those feelings to people who can serve as sources of support and validation, such as close friends, members of a support group, or a therapist. Ultimately, acceptance is the best way to reduce anger – acceptance of the past, acceptance of the present, and acceptance of the future. It can also be helpful to build one's spiritual health, through religious experience and observance or other spiritual means. Some people find meditation very effective in quieting anger and facilitating acceptance.

◆ **Guilt** can wreak havoc on a typical sibling's mind and heart. It often results from unresolved anger toward a sibling with ASD, or from life choices a typical sibling makes in his or her own best interests. Guilt in the context of this experience is inevitable, at least for some.

The important thing about guilt is to ensure that one does not drown in the emotion but is able to balance the guilt feelings with a sense of entitlement to one's own life. Even within the same family, typical siblings navigate the perilous waters of guilt differently. One sibling may feel mostly entitled to a life of his own, and only be minimally pulled into incorporating the needs of the sibling with ASD. Another may feel completely tied to the needs of the sibling with ASD and, therefore, be very challenged to contemplate her own independent needs and wants.

As with many other issues, there is not one correct path. Siblings must come to terms with what they can personally tolerate. Hopefully, this process will include sensitivity to the needs of the sibling with ASD and the larger family context, but how much and in what ways is as variable as people themselves. Those who are struggling intensely with guilt feelings, or who are torn between assisting their family of origin and building a life of their own, might be helped by making small changes rather than dramatic ones. For example, they might want to experiment with visiting every other week rather than every week. Tolerating a small change in the level of involvement is much easier than adapting to a radical shift. Furthermore, it will be easier for all involved parties if the changes are gradual. Another approach is for siblings to reflect on ways to substitute certain types of involvement for others. For example, perhaps they can read a monthly progress report instead of making a weekly call to the sibling's case manager. Finally, gradual shifts in levels of involvement enables typical siblings to slowly experiment with reduced levels of contact while evaluating how it makes them feel, how the rest of the family is reacting, and how to plan for future involvement.

◆ Typical siblings **worry** about their brother or sister with ASD in different ways across the life span. During the younger years, they may fear they will "catch" their brother or sister's problems. Later on, worries may center on how others will treat their brother or sister, or on unresolved issues of who will take care of the sibling with ASD in the future.

A good way to handle worry is to access available support by, for instance, discussing issues with parents or with other typical siblings. Just knowing that someone shares your concerns can go a long way toward ameliorating feelings of worry and creating workable solutions. Additionally, discussing issues with a trained counselor, for example, can clear up factual misconceptions, which are often at the root of a sibling's hidden worry.

◆ Having a sibling with ASD leads to **a sense of unfairness and loss**. Typical siblings may feel loss over their family's lack of spontaneity, resources, or both. Additionally, a typical sibling who has only one other sibling may feel the loss of a wished-for peer relationship in the family.

This is an area where acceptance becomes the goal. That is, we must relinquish our expectations in order to be able to accept what we have been given. With acceptance often comes the capacity for identifying "what is" as something to be cherished, instead of grieving for what could have been.

◆ The **limitations** posed by ASD can be very frustrating. A brother or sister's restricted ability to communicate, for example, may leave a typical sibling feeling largely left out of her brother or sister's life.

In such cases, it is helpful to learn more about how the sibling with autism best communicates and use the communication system of his choice. For example, if the individual with ASD uses signs, the typical sibling needs to learn them to effectively engage as a conversational partner. If the sibling with ASD uses the Picture Exchange Communication System, the typical sibling must be adept at using the system and ensuring it is accessible. It is also helpful to know the interests of the sibling. For example, it may be possible to have a very pleasant day bowling with the sibling or taking a ride on a train. Choosing activities that are of high interest and pleasurable for the person with ASD makes interactions much more successful and enjoyable.

◆ **Embarrassment** occurs in many contexts involving siblings with ASD, and is an emotion that just about every typical sibling encounters. Embarrassing feelings often linger in the minds of siblings, despite their attempts not to be embarrassed or efforts to "rise above it."

While embarrassment seems to be an inevitable experience for most siblings of people with ASD, the degree of embarrassment can be minimized. First, it is helpful to know that most outsiders operate from a position of ignorance when it comes to ASD. Few people know ASD and its impact the way a sibling does. Just knowing this can help mitigate feelings of discomfort. At times, it may be helpful to share information about the disability (see the suggestions in Appendix B), but this is a very personal choice and is not appropriate in every circumstance. Some family members find it helpful to create a mechanism for educating others about ASD. For example, in a difficult situation, they might explain to a curious onlooker or a critical commenter, "My brother has ASD. Here is a fact sheet about ASD." It might also help to educate the public about ASD in a more global way.

◆ Becoming **perfectionistic** and/or high achieving is one way some typical siblings try to compensate for their brother or sister's disability. Unfortunately, this reaction can create undue stress for the typical sibling or wrongly convey the notion to parents that the sibling has no legitimate needs of his own. Many typical siblings focus on accomplishing goals, performing well in school, and excelling in endeavors of their choice. They tend to adopt an independent stance, requiring little parental teaching, coaching, or attention. This often leads to positive accomplishments, strong friendships, and a sense of pride. In addition, it expands the world of the sibling, which can be very healthy and rewarding. Finally, it can be a great source of pride within the family, giving everyone something to celebrate and allowing the family to focus on achievements rather than the lack thereof.

Despite all the potential advantages, it is important that typical siblings not become so focused on independence and success that they fail to perceive their own right to attention. Parents must ensure that they remain available to the typical siblings and pay attention to them – not just contingent on their accomplishments, but unconditionally.

◆ Most typical siblings accept their brother or sister's disability, making peace with their situation and **finding ways to integrate** their sibling into their lives. Of course, the process of adjustment is influenced by the general atmosphere in the home. When things are calm, and there is no urgent crisis, adaptation is easier. It is difficult to achieve acceptance when the situation is unsafe, perennially challenging, or unremittingly sad.

What helps achieve stability? An appropriate placement of the family member with ASD goes a long way toward helping families achieve stability, particularly when it comes to challenging behaviors. Appropriate supports, including respite care and social outlets, may also help the family feel and behave in a more stable manner on a day-to-day basis. Further, good communication and strong relationships within the family help to ensure that members have access to supports when they most need them. With these foundations in place, it is possible to construct genuine relationships based on love and commitment.

◆ Typical siblings who grow up in a family marred by stress may end up with very **negative impressions of marriage and ever having a family** of their own. At times, these siblings express ambivalence toward or an avoidance of commitment. For example, they may choose a partner who is very needy emotionally or not truly capable of intimacy or reciprocity. Or siblings may perennially find themselves with partners who are unavailable or unsuitable. In most instances, these choices are not conscious; patterns of unsuccessful relationships simply emerge over time.

It is important for siblings to be honest with themselves about such patterns if positive changes are to be made. It is often helpful to seek counseling in an effort to understand and alter behavior. A therapist can help a person to acknowledge a pattern and identify any underlying fears of commitment and/or of marriage. Additionally, a therapist could challenge a person to behave differently (if there is a desire to change the pattern), and evaluate whether he or she is making better choices and altering old behavior patterns.

◆ Many siblings experience intense **fears of having a child of their own** with a disability. This is understandable and natural given the disability's presence in the family.

One way to allay such fears is to pursue genetic counseling. Genetic counselors and perinatologists are skilled in helping couples understand the range of risks, the options for genetic testing, and potential courses of action. Some genetic tests, such as those identifying Tay Sachs or cystic fibrosis, can be performed even before conception, and thus serve to reassure some anxious individuals. Other testing includes the triple-screen (alpha feto protein) blood test, which is done after the first trimester and can indicate an increased likelihood of neural tube defects (e.g., spina bifida) or Down's Syndrome. A more invasive, and perhaps risky, test is amniocentesis, which can detect

Down's Syndrome and other chromosomal abnormalities. While some individuals will want to pursue several or all of these tests, it should be noted that there is no way to detect autism in utero or determine an individual's particular level of risk for having a child with ASD.

◆ Some siblings might decide that the **genetic risk of autism** is too much and, therefore, forego the option of having children. Others proceed forward despite these fears. Both of these courses of action are legitimate and deeply personal.

Siblings who have chosen to have children can empower themselves by (a) learning more about the early signs and symptoms of ASD, (b) choosing a pediatrician with knowledge of developmental disabilities, (c) sharing the family's history of ASD with their physician, and (d) asking him or her to screen for ASD. These steps will help alleviate some anxiety. More important, increased knowledge and support will ensure that a sibling's own child will receive early diagnosis and intervention should symptoms of ASD arise.

According to the National Institute of Child Health and Human Development, **a doctor should promptly evaluate a child for autism if** he or she (a) does not babble or coo by 12 months; (b) does not gesture (point, wave, grasp) by 12 months; (c) does not say single words by 16 months; (d) does not say two-word phrases on his or her own by 24 months; and (e) has any loss of language or social skill at any age (National Institute of Child Health and Human Development, National Institutes of Health, "Autism Facts," NIH Pub. No. 01-4962, p. 5; June 2001).

◆ Many siblings find that they can fill perceived gaps in their immediate families by **developing special bonds with other relatives**. An aunt, an uncle, or a grandparent can provide individual attention, loving support, a helpful perspective, and opportunities for more diverse experiences. Often, siblings with access to such relationships later report how comforting they were. The adults in this context have a profound and lasting impact on the lives of typical siblings, and are associated with tremendous admiration and gratitude. It is imperative that all typical siblings have some of these special connections. If only one sibling has these types of experiences, it can lead the others to feel rejected or jealous.

Parents can foster such connections for their typical children, and encourage relatives to form special and close relationships with their children. Some siblings feel comfortable reaching out for this level of support on their own, but it is always helpful if adults take the lead. It might also be the case that a typical sibling forms a special connection with a family of relatives. Perhaps a certain aunt and uncle and their children create a unique connection with a typical sibling. This can have a very positive impact, as the typical sibling experiences life in a different family and a widening of perspective.

Chapter 5

The Affirmative Aspects: Finding Strength, Acceptance, and Compassion

M uch has been written, here and elsewhere, about the legitimate challenges faced by siblings of people with ASD. At the same time, it is important to remember that having a brother or sister with ASD can present opportunities for personal growth and development. In general, adults view the experience of having a sibling with a disability in positive terms. Over the years, the sting of embarrassment and the pain stemming from the perception of parental unfairness abate, at least for most siblings.

In this chapter, we focus on the ways in which having a brother or sister with ASD can help a typical sibling become strong, develop a sense of compassion toward others, and reach many positive goals in life.

A Sense of Mission

Many siblings of individuals with ASD find themselves drawn to the helping professions as a career. A sense of mission in improving the lives of those less fortunate leads them to focus on helping, teaching, and communicating with others. This is a natural and comfortable choice for many siblings whose experience of living with ASD sensitizes them to the world's need for love and kindness.

Anna Reed: What it's given me is that I can listen to clients [as a social worker] for hours and hours because I'm used to waiting! I'm patient and interested. When I got my master's in social work, a friend commented that when I was born they didn't say, "It's a girl," they said "It's a social worker!" I was born to heal and do family therapy.

My parents have taught me incredible values about taking care of people, and whether it's Joseph or a homeless man – there's this ethical value that it is our obligation, and also our honor, to take care of the downtrodden. Because of this I've been given this wonderful profession of therapist that comes totally naturally and makes me feel I have a purpose in life. It's made me a better person to be forced to see someone else's needs first.

Jessica Golden: When I was 14, I started being an aide in Sunday school for special needs kids. I did that for four years. I was a camp counselor too. I knew from an early age that I wanted to do something with special ed. I didn't know what.

Handicap issues have been in my life my whole life. Am I sick of it? No. I have a passion for legislation. I think it's really important. I feel like I have a lot to offer. When I die, I want to be known for something I did in this field.

The most positive thing I've learned from this is that you never give up on someone. I take so much of growing up with him to my job now. This was my dream to help people, and he helped me realize that dream.

Every year you get a couple of autistic kids and you can't give up because one of them could be a Will. And I really believe that. ...That one percent ... I think it's what keeps me going with my job, knowing that.

Bethany Powers: I don't know who I'd be without Emma. How would I be a writer without Emma? I wouldn't be the person I am. I like that person and feel protective of Emma and me.

Olivia Hanover: Autism is one of the reasons I became a special education teacher. I taught for 12 years before I had my son.

Jordan Cohen: I was elected to the Kansas state legislature when I was 27 and served for 11 years. When I talked about funding for people with disabilities, my life's experience added credibility. I would bring Marc to different functions, so my colleagues would see a face. I took the entire House and Senate to see *Rain Man*.

Marc's autism has given me insight and direction and focus in my life. I think I've been fortunate in what it's done for me. Marc has given me ambition, focus, and an understanding of people and their differences, capabilities, and disabilities. He has given me passion. Marc is every bit responsible for where I am as I am responsible for where I am.

Family and Personal Strength

Some of the siblings we spoke to attributed their sense of what is important in life to their family experience. For our interviewees, the importance of family was learned early on, in a gripping and genuine way. The experience was accompanied by a certain wisdom and strength, as siblings learned the powerful solidifying effects of adversity and how to advocate for a loved one. These are lessons that many do not learn until well into adulthood and that create a perspective that is older and wiser than age and experience might imply.

Olivia Hanover: I learned a lot from my mom. Her children always came first. She's helped me out a great deal throughout all this [her son's diagnosis]. She shows me where to find strength at times in different things. To look at the whole picture and not little bits and pieces. My nuclear family was always very positive. I try to find the best in any situation. Adversity has taught me never to say never.

Sometimes there's a reason for this that we don't know. For everything there is a reason. As tough as it was on all of us, especially my parents, it showed that they had a rock-solid marriage and that's why they're still together. He is the root that keeps us together. To this day, any of us would do anything when it comes to Matthew.

Julie Shore: If it weren't for Robby, I wouldn't have learned at a young age how to cope with problems.

Dana Peters: Chris has brought us closer in a way you can't describe. He's just brought us closer together. He's the focus of our family, basically, in terms of how we think. He's the glue, and he's shaped how my sister and I think and act. You can't separate the person I am – or my sister – from my brother.

True colors come through in times of adversity. Adversity has taught me not to take things for granted, like my health. It's most important to be strong during adverse times.

Michael Stern: Rich's experience has taught me the meaning of family and one's commitments to the family. I can only now confront my shame and self-hatred after so many years. I've grown to learn things about myself in many ways for the positive. I have become a good father and husband and put family ahead of all else.

Looking back on our family experience, I know now how Rich taught us all to be strong during hard times and to not take the seemingly important items of the day-to-day life so seriously.

Sarah Cooper: I witnessed a lot of situations with my mother, who is very good at public relations. She was trying to get Rick an education, and at the time, our township wouldn't pay for pretoddler special ed. She championed his cause, and I saw my mother become very politically active and I learned things through her talking to the media and other people. I was proud; it was something unique.

When I was pregnant, I had no doubt about my parenting skills. I came into motherhood feeling pretty confident, and a lot of that had to do with my brother.

Ashley Williams: Once a parent called Todd a bully and I turned to the person and told her he couldn't help it, he had autism. I was 10 at the time and scared to death, yet I did it anyway because Todd can't stand up for himself. That's something I need, have, and want to do for him.

Susan Peters: Adversity has taught me not to stress about minor things. [Chris has] taught me that things don't have to be so complicated. He's taught me to see what's important in life.

Lynne Stern Feiges: Rich has taught my whole family how to be strong in the face of adversity. There's always been this strong loyalty between us, and I think it comes from Rich. When my daughter was hospitalized for seizures at the age of one, I drew on the strength I developed from knowing Rich. It was kind of this "back against the wall" feeling that seemed all too familiar to me. Another thing I've learned about adversity is that one defense is to maintain your sense of humor. One night we went to visit Rich at the institution, which is understandably like a prison, with locked doors and elevators, guards, the whole works. When we got to his wing and asked to see him, the guard bellowed out "Mr. Richard Stern" down this dingy hallway. The sounds just echoed off the walls, and then Rich started scuffling toward us in his dirty clothes. My mother and I whispered to each other, "It's like Dead Man Walking!" I mean, totally not funny, but if we didn't have a laugh at that moment, we would have fallen apart.

Bethany Powers: I don't know if Emma was meant to be who she is. I can't answer that question, I'm not God. But I was meant to be Emma's sister. What moral fiber I have has been formed around my sister, around learning that I didn't walk away from her. That I loved her and that I could become friends with her. That I could take care of her and leave her free.

Moments of Joy and Pride

Joy and pride are part of the experience of most families, including those in which there is a member with ASD. The typical siblings we spoke to experienced great joy in many contexts with their sibling with ASD. For example, siblings reported enjoying finding activities they could share with their brother or sister. This is tremendously important, as bonds are built and strengthened through time spent together and through shared experiences. Typical siblings also relished seeing their sibling with ASD succeed and accomplish things. There was a special understanding of the sometimes grand efforts that led to successes, and typical siblings enthusiastically cheered and celebrated those. Typical siblings also appreciated the positive personality traits of their sibling with ASD. In some ways, this reflected the essence of true connectedness, as siblings saw their brother or sister not just as a person with ASD, but as someone with unique qualities, interests, and humor.

Jeremy Plant: Eli and I do a lot of things. He's into buses, and sometimes we'll go on rides throughout the city.

Last year [our team] played a baseball game about two hours away from here. My dad and Eli drove up. When a foul ball was hit out of the park, the concession stand gave out 50 cents for every returned foul ball. [Eli] ended up with $15 bucks on the day! He was all proud of it, and it was so cute!

I looked at his report card last time – I never did before – and I was impressed. It wasn't good grades or anything and, granted, he did receive a lot of help, but hey, it doesn't matter. It doesn't say that on the report card.

Sometimes when I go out for a jog, I take him with me. I can't go real fast. ... I have to just keep up. If he lags behind, I'll sprint for about 20 feet, turn around, and he always comes. Sometimes he'll fall flat on the ground and say, "Jeremy, carry me home!" It's kind of hard to do that!

Jessica Golden: Will is a great brother. He's a really nice guy. He'd do anything for you. If I needed something, he'd do anything for me and would be there in a second. He's friendly. He doesn't always know what to say, but he'll go up to anyone and say "Hi, I'm Will." That's the way he is. On our wedding video, he was the one leading the conga line! That's Will!

I'm very proud of Will. The fact that people were so mean to him and he still plugged on. He's had so many achievements. Even though he had to take some things three or four times, now he's getting a master's.

Sarah Cooper: When I had my daughter, everyone was interested in seeing what Rick's reaction would be. This was the big question. When he saw her, there was no reaction. I don't know what we were hoping for, but it was a little disappointing. Now I'll ask him what the baby's name is and he'll tell me. I'll take it!

For me, it's a positive experience. I pick him up every weekend, cook whatever he wants. It's a little bit of spoiling, but who doesn't like that?

Ashley Williams: Todd contributes so much to the family, it is impossible to say everything. His best characteristic is his personality. He is almost always smiling or laughing. He'll approach me and ask for tickles or a hug, or chase me. I love Todd very much and he is one of, if not the most, cherished relationships in my life.

Richard Flynn: He's my best friend ... Sometimes we wrestle and watch TV.

Maryann Hall: One of the best parts is that I get a lot of free stuff through her [activities], like programs at the farms.

Bethany Powers: Emma works for a candy company packaging candy. It's part time, but she likes her job and it fits in with her view of herself, which is "I'm a child." She has this view of herself, and around this she has constructed a world in which she is actually independent. She pays her bills by going to the bank and getting money orders. She won't get a checking account.

She occasionally comes out with something so straightforward and correct that it strikes me like a thunderbolt. We were one time talking about our parents, about their being away, and I mentioned that one day they are going to die, and Emma said, "I'll miss them." Time and again she will come out with these things. It's grounding to me.

She tries hard to be a good sister to me. We have learned to say "I love you" to each other. I know I mean it, and I believe she does too. It's been a long process of 10 years trying to become close. Emma holds up her end. She's not as strong as I am.

Dana Peters: We always joke that if he weren't autistic, he'd be the smartest one out of us. One time, I hurt myself and was bleeding all over the house. He cut himself one day and immediately put pressure on himself! He's got this sixth sense and knows what to do. He's also very aware of emotions in the room. If someone's upset or about to cry, he'll say, "It's alright, it's alright." Or, he'll think he's getting into trouble, and say, "I'm sorry." He can sense tension, whether it's anger or sadness. Whenever there's chaos or any break to the status quo, he'll sense that right away.

When he was 13, he went to my high school graduation. He sat through the whole thing and that was a huge deal. It was important for me to have him there, and it was important for my parents to go together as a family. That was like, "yeah!"

Susan Peters: Chris has an understanding of death. We had an uncle that died, and he became more affectionate to show that he was supportive.

There was a bowling tournament that he did through school. I went with him, and it was really special because he always came to our games. Another defining moment was when I taught my brother to slow dance at a party. He got up to dance with me. Now at parties, he initiates it, and he won't let me sit down! He's a party animal! That's another thing, his sense of humor. He always brings my spirits up. He's got a great, fun-loving personality. And he's a really hard worker, which I admire about him. He's very caring and loving and can show it.

Lynne Stern Feiges: When you think of a person with autism, you generally picture someone who is detached from others. It's never been that way with Rich and me. We've always had this strong connection to each other, and there have been moments of camaraderie, despite all the worry and sadness I have about him. I once took him to my apartment in college to make spaghetti and hang out with my roommates. He still asks me to go there (and I have to explain to him that I now live 3,000 miles away!). We also slow danced at my wedding. But the best by far was when my daughter was born, and he looked at her and said, "Coochie Coo, you have a beautiful baby!" He even learned her name and gave us a present.

Jordan Cohen: After my fianceé died, Marc asked the rabbi, "When will I die?" I've never heard an autistic talk about death. It spooked me.

Marc can dress himself, but he doesn't always match. He likes to go shopping and can fix himself some food. His most significant achievement has been living in this apartment and working at the recycling center. Going out into the community, living semi-independently, accepting the "march of life and death" that happens to every family.

When I was in the legislature, I went to an Association of Retarded Citizens reception with Marc. I'm walking around the room extending my hand to people and saying, "I'm Representative Cohen." Marc was right behind me saying, "I'm Marc Cohen, I'm Marc Cohen." That was so precious and pretty amazing.

Jamie Cohen: Marc has a sense of humor. He makes puns, and a lot of what he does almost runs to slapstick. He really enjoys kid movies like *Home Alone*, where someone's always throwing something. He'll always repeat and bring up funny things that happened with us years later.

Lance Strong: It gives us a lot of satisfaction to see him do well and to learn new things. He's saying a few words now. We wrestle sometimes. [Do you let him win?] No, I'm not gonna let him win!

Michael Stern: Rich displayed some lucid observations at timely moments that were amazing and humorous, allowing us to feel that he was "just like us." Rich's bar mitzvah was the greatest achievement, by far and away. Nobody ever dreamed he could do it.

Compassion and Patience

The experience of living with and loving a person with ASD is life-changing. It alters one's perspective in a permanent way and shapes the development of one's values. Our interviewees universally referred to an opening of the heart and mind. Siblings are less judgmental and more open to diversity in the appearance and behavior of others. They feel compassion for the struggles of others and are patient. They can wait as someone struggles to communicate, to move, or whatever. They want to help others, and are nurturing and caring souls. They are this way, in part, because of their love for a brother or sister with autism. They have seen difference and have embraced it. They have seen struggle and have nurtured and assisted it. They know about the complexities of life and about the challenges that face individuals with disabilities. For the most part, they strive to make the lives of others softer, sweeter, and better.

Jeremy Plant: I think I have a greater appreciation not only for life, but for people in general. It used to be a joke to make fun of disabled people walking down the street. But I was always like, "Don't make fun of them, they are people, too, and there's nothing they can do about it." You accept a lot more things. You see people and you think, wow, why couldn't this have been my brother, but then I realize, well, I wouldn't trade him in. He's my brother.

Becky Lott: We have a few handicapped people at work, and I think I have a lot more patience with them because of living with Gordon. Most people don't, because they don't know how to deal with them.

Sarah Cooper: Because of Rick, I'm a lot more patient, sympathetic toward other people. I don't make a lot of judgments. It's not something I can state directly, it's more of a feeling inside. It's basically about love.

Dana Peters: Chris has given me a broader perspective. I can relate to different people, and he has taught me to be more accepting.

Susan Peters: Chris has made me more patient, sensitive, caring, and nurturing. My relationship has made those traits grow in me. I kind of felt different than some of my friends because I kind of had that caretaker role in some ways. That's something my friends didn't have growing up. I think autism's caused me to put a lot of people's needs first. It's something that I struggle with. I want to help people, but sometimes I have a hard time meeting my own needs and saying no to things.

I can't see myself not working with people, not helping people. In particular, people who have problems.

Leslie Cohen: Marc makes me more understanding, patient, and caring toward others. I think if I had children of my own, I would have been a good parent. Though, perhaps, if I were younger, I'd have been overprotective.

Jordan Cohen: I don't view my life as being painful or tragic. My mother didn't view life this way either. I view it all as a blessing that's made me more conscious of other people's pain. More empathetic about what other people go through.

Jamie Cohen: Marc has made me more sensitive to people who need more – to their feelings, which they have like everyone else. Whatever joy they get in their life is just as important as what any "normal" person gets in their life.

Ashley Williams: I am a much more patient person than most of my friends. Also, I'm not as prejudiced and a lot more open-minded than them. I also tend to be more bossy, mother-like, and responsible than my friends just because of the way I act with Todd.

Lynne Stern Feiges: Rich enabled me to realize that things don't have to be normal and perfect to be OK. I don't strive to have that perfect "magazine life." I have a stronger threshold for people's imperfections.

Situations and Solutions

◆ Life experiences, including both our triumphs and our struggles, all influence who we are and how we see ourselves. Many typical siblings **see themselves as good at what they do**, particularly in the realms of caring for others and communicating. They also see themselves as more mature than their peers, which is understandable given the range of experiences they usually have. For example, some have been exposed to health care professionals to a much greater extent than is usually the case for young people, and some have been exposed to serious conversations within the family from an early age. On the positive side, this has the effect of increasing one's self-concept, but it may also become a barrier to developing peer relationships. Typical siblings may feel that they lack common ground because they have experiences that are far different from the majority of kids they meet growing up. At times, a typical sibling may grow too comfortable in the role of a serious observer, failing to pursue the more frivolous and fun experiences of life.

For these reasons, it is a good idea for siblings to form relationships with others in a similar circumstance, not only because of the common experiences, but because they can help each other to balance the serious and spontaneous sides of life. Parents, too, can help siblings to balance these two very different experiences and needs. Perhaps the best way is to be conscious of the need for a balanced life. Thus, parents can self-monitor their own communications to ensure that worry and negativity do not obscure the joy and delight. In other words, parents are powerful models of how to live, and of how to balance the good and the bad, the wonderful and the challenging parts of every life.

◆ The experience of having a sibling with ASD influences myriad areas of a typical sibling's life, most particularly **career**

choices. Many typical siblings pursue the helping professions – a logical and comfortable choice given the first-hand knowledge they usually have of the value of bettering other people's lives. Sibling involvement in the helping professions is also often a reflection of the caretaking role they have always had.

Understandably, some typical siblings wish to avoid these professions in an effort to differentiate their professional experiences from their personal lives. Siblings must realize that this is completely acceptable and does not mean that opportunities for helping are diminished. For example, a typical sibling who chooses to go into business may remain very committed to improving a brother or sister's life and circumstances by, say, establishing fund-raising or other programs that suit his or her needs. Siblings torn between career choices must soul-search about their path. A sibling's career choice should reflect a true desire for a particular professional identity – not serve as compensation for guilty feelings about what the sibling has or has not done for a brother or sister with ASD.

◆ Given that bonds between people are built through interactions and shared experiences, a good goal for a typical sibling is to **discover ways to spend time** doing enjoyable things with a brother or sister with ASD. This is sometimes a challenge, as typical siblings may not know how to build these bridges or may feel thwarted by their brother or sister's disruptive or rigid behavior. Many typical siblings in this situation simply give up, despite a desire to find common ground. But some simple strategies may make the process of interacting much more effective for all parties.

Siblings of any age can be helped by simply learning more about what their brother or sister enjoys. This may require contacting the people who work every day with the sibling with ASD, as they often possess the best information about that sibling's favorite foods, activities, and interests.

Adolescent siblings may want to participate in a sibling training program offered by their brother or sister's school or a
local autism agency. These programs teach skills for communicating with people with ASD, such as ensuring attention to
what is said and reinforcing positive behavior, which can go a
long way toward increasing successful interactions. As a family moves through the various life cycles, typical siblings
should realize that the degree of interaction they have with
their brother or sister with ASD will ebb and flow.

◆　Because autism is a spectrum disorder, there is tremendous
variability in the **achievement levels** of individuals with
ASD. While some people with ASD have severe disabilities,
others are only mildly impacted by their disability. Thus, the
range of what is possible for people with ASD is enormous, and varying levels of achievement can translate to
stellar accomplishments for different individuals. Typical siblings told us of the great pride and joy they felt watching
what their sibling was able to do, despite whatever limitations he or she might have. For example, they recognized
the sometimes monumental efforts involved in learning to
write, in speaking in sentences, in writing a poem, in taking
a bus, in applying for a job, in making a cake, in going to college. This recognition enabled the typical sibling to both
accept – without resignation – what their brother or sister
could not do and to rejoice in what was possible for them.

How does one achieve acceptance and capacity for
joy? The siblings we spoke to did not discuss struggling to
achieve this. Rather, it seems to have evolved over a life-
time of assisting and witnessing the capabilities and challenges faced by their sibling with ASD. Thus, the more typical siblings know about and see the abilities and struggles
of their sibling with ASD, the more active they can be as
cheerleaders and celebrants.

◆ It seems like such a cliché to discuss strength as a conse-quence of **adversity**. And yet, over and over in our inter-views, siblings attributed their personal and familial strength to having experienced the hardship that is inherent in a fami-ly living with ASD. Of course, people differ in their approach to adversity; that is, each of us brings an intrinsic sense of optimism or pessimism to our circumstances.

Nevertheless, it cannot be overstated how much of an impact optimism, or learned optimism, can have on a family living with ASD. Among other things, optimistic families are more inclined to learn how to manage challenging behaviors effectively, to seek out appropriate services, or to advocate for their loved one. Sometimes optimism is learned from parents who model such behavior. Where this is not the case, siblings may ultimately be able to overcome adversity by learning to identify challenges, avoiding unnecessary drama, and maintaining a problem-solving approach when stress seems overwhelming.

◆ Perhaps the most striking and prevalent quality of siblings of people with ASD is their **increased capacity for com-passion and patience**. Often, this is a very global quality, something siblings bring to every interaction. For example, it is easy for many typical siblings to wait until someone has finished talking, even when they are long-winded or a bit tangential. It is also often easy for them to wait as someone counts change at an achingly slow pace when in line at a supermarket. These types of things – for which most peo-ple often have little tolerance – are effortless to many sib-lings of people with ASD, most likely as an inescapable con-sequence of growing up with someone with ASD.

Certainly, the world would be a kinder place if such qualities were more widespread. Perhaps the movement toward having more people with disabilities integrated into general education and larger community activities will result in patience and compassion on a grander scale.

Chapter 6

Coping Strategies: Managing Sibling Effects of ASD

As we have seen in the previous discussion and the first-hand accounts presented, being a sibling of a person with ASD creates stress. What, then, can a typical sibling do to handle this stress? The first step, we believe, is to understand the nature of stress. Then, it is helpful to adopt strategies for combating stress, particularly as it relates to having a sibling with a disability.

In this chapter, we will first discuss what the experts say about stress, and about how it can be managed. Then we will turn to the siblings we interviewed to see what coping strategies they employ.

Stress

Stress has been defined as any circumstance in which demands exceed resources and, alternately, as any circumstance requiring adjustment or adaptation. The literature on stress helps us to understand the types of experiences that are especially difficult to cope with. For example, stressors that are of a long duration are more difficult to adapt to than those of a short-term nature. (It is more difficult to prepare oneself for a marathon than for a sprint!) Families with a person with ASD are in it for the long haul and, therefore, are prone to stress.

We also know that the ambiguity of a stressor increases negative effects. One can hardly get more ambiguous than ASD. It is difficult for families to predict the course of ASD, the prognosis for the affected individual, his or her daily behavior, the permanence of a placement, or the long-term needs of the family member with ASD.

Finally, we know that the degree to which a stressor distinguishes us from our peers adds to its effects. Most parents of children with ASD feel that their experiences are unique and dramatically different from those of their family and friends (Marsh, 1993), as reflected in a sense of isolation (Seligman & Darling, 1997). Similarly, most siblings of people with ASD feel quite different from their peers while growing up. For example, their families must consider many things that other families cannot even imagine, such as long-term care, separation from a sibling during childhood, and use of unusual or aversive treatment methods.

Furthermore, as adults, typical siblings often assume a level of responsibility for their brother or sister with ASD that is not part of the typical sibling experience. This circumstance can lead to a sense of isolation, and even to depression.

The nature of ASD creates unique stress as well compared to other disabilities. For example, mothers of children with ASD reportedly experience more stress than mothers of children with mental retardation (Donovan, 1988) or children with cystic fibrosis, a chronic and fatal illness (Bouma & Schweitzer, 1990). Many children with ASD are aloof or avoidant of attempts at affection, which may help explain the increased stress. In addition, mothers of children with ASD have a consistent stress profile (Koegel et al., 1992), characterized by concerns over child dependency and limitations on family activities. Fathers and mothers both express concerns about their child's independence and acceptance in the community (Moes, Schreibman, & Loos, 1992; Rodrigue, Morgan, & Geffken, 1990). Finally, concern for the future is especially acute in these families.

Siblings are not immune to these concerns, and are sensitized to them over time. Indeed, siblings report that these concerns surface early in life. There is always a sense that their brother or sister will need more support than they will. Often, there is also an understanding that this extra support must come from them, both while their parents can care for their sibling and after they are no longer able to do so.

Support from Others

What do we know about buffers against stress for these families? The significance of social support, such as being listened to, understood, or being helped in some concrete way, has been demonstrated repeatedly (e.g., Boyce, Behl, Mortensen, & Akers, 1991; Byrne & Cunningham, 1985; Johnson & Sarason, 1978; McCubbin, 1979). For example, in a series of studies of mothers of children with ASD, Bristol and Schropler (1983) found that women experiencing the least stress were receiving the greatest support, particularly from spouses and relatives. Nothing is lonelier than traveling a difficult path alone. Even when we must ultimately meet challenges largely by ourselves, we feel less alone if we can share the experience with others and if we feel understood by others.

Support from partners has a particularly powerful buffering effect (Kazak & Marvin, 1984; Turnbull & Turnbull, 1990). Although in traditional families much of the burden in decision making and in daily life falls on mothers, fathers play a central role, and their attitudes and openness can help the family cope more effectively. For example, it may be helpful for a father to have a weekly outing with the child with ASD and/or with typical siblings, to not only interact with his children, but also to provide respite for the mother. In addition, some families find it helpful to identify indirectly supportive behaviors that decrease stress, such as driving the mother to meetings, cleaning the house, or going food shopping.

Siblings are often in a peculiar position when it comes to support. Like their parents, they need support themselves. Like their parents, their experiences are very different from those of others. A typical sibling looking at other kids and other families on the block often feels very unusual. So where does a sibling's support come from? In childhood, parents provide the most essential and most influential support. Other adults who can provide support may include grandparents, aunts and uncles, teachers, and clergy. Other children usually don't provide such support, unless they are in a similar situation (such as through a sibling support group).

Experiences vary, depending on whether there is only one typical sibling or several. As mentioned earlier, large families offer some protection from the negative impact of a family member with disabilities (Siegel & Silverstein, 1994). This may be because there is less contact between siblings or fewer comparisons between each sibling and the child with a disability. It may also be that responsibilities are more evenly distributed across more players in the family. Furthermore, more typical siblings in a family also means more potential sources of support for each member of the family.

As siblings age, they are more likely to get their emotional and social needs met through a variety of sources, often outside the immediate family. Even so, siblings report that they do not always get much support from friends (Siegel & Silverstein, 1994). It is common for siblings to feel inhibited about sharing many details of their brother or sister's ASD with friends. Secrecy and embarrassment are prevalent. Moreover, it is rare for siblings to feel that their friends truly understand the impact of having a brother or sister with ASD, particularly in terms of how it affects life choices or long-term planning. It is simply the case that siblings with such a brother or sister "grow up" fast, in terms of understanding what caring for a loved one who is not independent involves. These are lessons many don't learn until a parent ages or until they bear a child of their own.

Support from spouses can also be difficult to obtain. While many spouses are welcoming of the sibling with a disability, some feel resentment about the roles and responsibilities that come with the territory. Even when a spouse has not expressed any negative feelings, some siblings fear this and want to protect their spouse from too much stress stemming from their sibling with ASD.

A less emotional and more consistent source of social support comes from professionals. Thus, families of children with ASD have long benefited from a variety of formal support services from professionals (Farran & Sparling, 1988; Honig & Winger, 1997). These include parent training programs, parent support groups, family therapy, and individual therapy.

Siblings might participate in professionally facilitated activities such as sibling support groups or sibling skill training programs. These programs offer opportunities to feel less alone and to build skills that make siblings more effective in interacting with their brother or sister with ASD. Some siblings also participate in individual or family therapy as children as a way to alleviate some global familial stress and bring previously hidden issues to the forefront.

It is of interest that the perceived availability of social support seems to be a crucial variable in coping with stress (Wolf et al., 1989). This makes sense. If we feel we have someone who could provide assistance if we need it, we feel less isolated. In fact, it may matter more that you can envision telling someone the story of a very stressful day than whether anyone helps you through that day in a concrete way. Thus, siblings might just want to tell a friend about a horrendous trip to the supermarket, where a sibling with ASD overturned carts and people were staring. They don't need help in a concrete way, but they want someone to validate their embarrassment and the trauma.

"My Uncle Bob got it. He knew that my parents sometimes missed the boat, and he knew that my sister would be useless. Somehow, it helped just to know he understood. He wasn't going to change a thing, but he could witness the chaos and listen when I needed to vent."

Those who feel most alone are individuals who cannot think of someone they would call to listen to a story of family squabbling, to help them decide between two possible residential placements, or to provide some "babysitting" support for a sibling at a large family event. We need to feel that there are people who are there for us, who will lend a hand, who will take the time to hear our tales, and who will care about the outcomes of our decisions.

Coping always involves personal initiative, whether someone is lucky enough to have ample social support or not. Let us examine some of the ways in which people can focus on making positive changes in the midst of stress.

Coping Strategies

Coping strategies refer to deliberate efforts made to alleviate the distress associated with a particular stressor (Cohen & Lazarus, 1979; Lazarus & Folkman, 1984). One type of coping strategy, instrumental coping, focuses on implementing change directly in persons or in the environment, and would include, in this context, parent skill training programs or informational programs. A lot has been written about the helpfulness of instrumental coping strategies for families of people with ASD, but much of it focuses on the parents or the family as a whole (e.g., Bristol, 1985, 1986; Harris, 1983, 1984), not siblings in particular.

Parents have been helped immensely by parent training programs and a variety of activities and programs that increase knowledge and skills about ASD. But not all of the positive effects of such strategies are related to increasing skills or knowledge; participation in this kind of activity itself reduces the degree of stress experienced.

Similarly, siblings might engage in a variety of informational or instructional activities that increase skills and reduce stress. For example, a sibling might take a class or a workshop on ways to effectively communicate with, teach, or reward a person with ASD. Such workshops may be available at statewide autism conferences or through an advocacy and information organization. Additionally, a sibling might take a class in generic stress management. Such classes are often offered by local organizations that advertise in the community or through community colleges. Alternately, a sibling might take a seminar in estate planning. Any of these activities could be instrumental coping strategies. As is the case for parents, these options represent a way to increase one's skills while at the same time reducing stress. Becoming involved in this kind of activity also adds to an overall sense of "doing something" useful about the issues, and in that way, is empowering. It is the opposite of simply wondering, waiting, or idly feeling ineffective.

Families of children with ASD have also been helped by the use of palliative coping strategies such as holding philosophically comforting views of life and searching for satisfaction in areas of life other than the child with a disability (Albanese, Miguel, & Koegel, 1996; Bristol & Schopler, 1983). These types of strategies do not have a direct impact on the environment. Rather, they are more of an internal coping mechanism, facilitating adjustment and fostering the ability to cope.

Using this approach, some families find it useful to focus on all of the ways in which having a person with a disability has altered their perspectives. For example, it may have helped them to value life and happiness over the objective achievements someone can reach. Other families are comforted in a religious or spiritual sense by finding meaning. That is, they may feel that there is a reason for their experience of disability – that there is a spiritual purpose to the experience that goes beyond what we can easily comprehend. Some families find it helpful to develop a completely different interest, such as having a family band or going camping. What these strategies have in common is that they help families to feel comfort, to experience joy, and to find meaning in living day to day.

"I don't have a support group, though that would be nice. But it is good to know that other families struggle with the same kinds of issues that my family struggles with. I mean, we don't have horns on our heads, but I sometimes felt like we do. Now I know other families have horns on their heads, too!"

What about siblings?

Siblings also develop palliative coping strategies. Presumably, they are often helped by the strategies that were adopted in their families of origin. Thus, many of the siblings we spoke to told us that they had developed a sense of mission. Some developed a broad sense of mission about helping others, others became focused on ASD. Some developed a specific and personal sense of mission, viewing it as an important part of their destiny to help make their brother or sister's life better. Many siblings also reported a shift in perspectives and values, viewing themselves as substantially different from how they would have been without their sibling with ASD. These are all ways in which people find meaning, reasons for joy, and the capacity for hope and healing in a less than perfect world.

A person's beliefs, attitudes, perceptions, and values can mitigate feelings of victimization, hopelessness, and helplessness. Over and over again this was reflected in our interviews. As highlighted in Chapter 5, many of our interviewees reported experiencing a positive impact of having a sibling with ASD. For example, many found great meaning, a sense of purpose, an enhanced capacity for compassion, or a more global sense of obligation to those who need and require support in various ways. Many of the siblings viewed themselves as better people than they might have been without the presence of their sibling with ASD in their life.

Nevertheless, siblings also told us about isolation and the need for support. Some needed more support than others. Some found it readily, others had to pay professionals to get appropriate and adequate support. Regardless, what is important is the recognition that stress requires support; it is the nature of the human condition. It is not heroic to cope alone; it is unnatural. Coping with an extraordinary stressful circumstance without support is not possible. While we may be able to do it for a while, it will catch up with us in the form of physical ailments or psychological issues. The physical and emotional consequences of stress are real and must be dealt with. Every person with a brother or sister with ASD has an untold story, and each of their stories is a story of stress and a story of coping.

Our interviewees told us a lot about how they managed the stress of their experience. Here are some of the themes that emerged in their responses.

- **Get support from people in similar situations.** Siblings generally reported that support from others in similar situations was immensely helpful. No one can understand what it is like to be a sibling of a person with ASD quite like another sibling of a person with autism can. Some siblings are lucky to receive such support from within their own families. Others benefit from friends and contacts who share this life circumstance. These may be found either through Internet organizations such as Sibnet, or through a national or state organization that assists with networking (see Appendix C). Either way, it helps to reduce isolation.

- **Communicate honestly and openly.** The extent to which families can openly discuss the issues of future planning and problem solving greatly affects how severe the negative effects of stress are. In families where these issues can be directly addressed, adaptation is reportedly better. In addition, when siblings themselves can honestly discuss their preferred levels of involvement, they report less distress over such issues.

Some of the siblings we interviewed gave us specific suggestions for how to increase communication within the family. Some families held regular family meetings to discuss issues surrounding the child with ASD as a forum for addressing concerns over inequities, schedules for friends to visit, and problem solving for various upcoming events. Many siblings told us of the benefit of learning to speak their mind, to express an opinion. A sibling might feel that the family needed a respite weekend or a night out each week without the child with ASD. Or a sibling might be convinced that a certain residential placement appeared inhumane. A sibling might want to participate more actively by becoming involved with a service provider, helping plan the annual picnic, or volunteering once a month at a recreational program. Over and over again, our interviewees told us that speaking the truth in these matters helped them feel personally better and helped the family function more effectively.

> *"Everyone needs a good friend, or two or three. Hey, no one ever really walks in your pair of shoes, and that's not what it's about. But everyone has challenges, everyone feels alone, and everyone gets discouraged sometimes."*

- **Talk about the future.** Future planning also requires attention. One sibling had a "what if" file that listed who to be called and what needed to be done in a variety of unlikely, yet possible, circumstances. While those circumstances might be different across families, they could include the death of a parent, the loss of a vocational or residential placement, a severe behavioral escalation, or a hospitalization.

  Similarly, many siblings reported deriving solace from developing a "game plan." This could include the explicit assignment of current and future roles. Who will be the family liaison for staff members working with the sibling? Who will talk to medical doctors? Who will be the legal guardian? Who will visit the sibling, and how often? How will holidays be dealt with? The extent to which the family can be up-front and direct about planning for the future has an impact on the typical sibling's levels of distress. Generally, it is better to know than it is to wonder.

- **Seek professional help.** Some siblings told us that the judicious use of formal supports, such as individual, group, or family therapy, was extremely helpful. When it is not possible to address issues adequately alone, it is better to enlist the support of a therapist than to suffer silently. Guilt and anger are the two emotions that siblings struggled with most intensely, and are the emotions that often prevented them from realizing their own potential in a variety of ways. Anger, in particular, is insidious. It tends to cloud our views, alter our capacity for joy, and prevent us from being fully present in the moment. Guilt, too, prevents us from feeling free to pursue goals, to experience joy, and to move ahead. According to our interviewees, leaving guilt and anger behind freed them in immeasurable ways, and enabled them to create healthy relationships both within and outside their families of origin.

- **Have a healthy sense of entitlement.** Our interviewees seemed to be helped by a sense of entitlement to personal happiness, to an independent life, to some freedom from the constant demands of caretaking they may have seen their parents assume. Imposing some limits on their level of involvement or responsibility not only helped typical siblings to balance their own needs versus those of the family, it sometimes helped the family as a whole to adapt or the sibling with ASD to achieve more independence.
    In any case, it was often imperative for siblings to figure out their own minds and hearts regarding what level of responsibility was comfortable. Is a visit to the residence fine, but overnights at their own home not? Is it okay to track finances, but not to be the legal guardian?

Is it comfortable to talk to medical doctors, but not to attend annual goal meetings? These are questions that have no right or wrong answers and, therefore, must be answered on an individual basis.

- **Develop a personal sense of faith.** Spirituality has long been associated with helping people to adapt to stress and to meet the demands of extraordinarily difficult circumstances. While some siblings expressed this in religious or philosophical terms, others discussed more simple and concrete spiritual acts. Some siblings reported that they found it helpful to read inspirational stories, to meditate, or to volunteer with those less fortunate.

- **Maintain hope.** Our interviewees had much to mourn and many problems to face on a daily basis.

"I remember when my family went to see a therapist. It was the first time I could talk about how embarrassed I was to have my friends over. I thought everyone could see how unfair that was, and I guess I thought they didn't care. But talking as a family helped me see that everyone was just too busy to notice."

The capacity to hope may have been the most important resource they brought to the challenge. Some people have proposed that the difference between sadness and depression is the presence of hope in sadness. Despair is truly the absence of hope. The siblings we interviewed had much to be sad about, but also much to hope for.

A pervasive optimism, which has been globally associated with positive adaptation (Seligman, 1991), helped them to view their own situation and that of their siblings in a positive light. Many siblings came to optimism only after weathering some rough storms with their sibling. They may have seen institutionalization, a psychiatric collapse, or the loss of a placement that appeared to be permanent. They may have truly feared that their sibling and their family would not be able to endure such experiences. In retrospect and from safer ground, they can often see that it was possible to cope with and transcend such experiences. They may even report that a "catastrophe" opened better options, forced the family to work effectively toward a better solution, or led to improved treatment.

Many of the siblings we spoke with viewed their circumstances not only with a positive stance, but with humor and even with joy. Thus, many of them were characterized by the capacity to laugh in the face of a chronic stressor and the ability to experience joy amid disappointment. These were people who had seen darkness, and who knew that light would appear again. They cherished the light, nurtured it, and helped it to grow.

"It really helped me to see a therapist. I resolved my anger about my situation, about my lot in life, so to speak. I was angry at everyone at one time, and it kept me from being happy. I needed help to leave it behind."

Conclusion

What Does It All Mean?

So what does it mean to have a brother or sister with ASD? As we have seen in the preceding chapters, it means different things to different people, yet commonalities emerged.

Above all, it means having a different kind of a life, a life that is discrepant from that of one's peers. It also means living in a family faced with unique challenges, especially compared with those faced by most other families. It means coping with different pressures when making life choices, such as where to live or whether to have children. Most people do not experience the same degrees of ambivalence over pursuing independent lives or about starting a family of their own.

Additionally, having a sibling with ASD can result in powerful negative emotions that are sometimes hard to admit and deal with. A sibling's unusual and stigmatizing behaviors can be embarrassing. Wishing that a sibling with a disability was not part of the family may reflect a typical sibling's true feelings but can also lay the foundation for intractable guilt.

And yet, anyone growing up with a brother or sister with ASD will tell you that a lot of good can come from this kind of adversity. Strength, compassion, and tolerance are some of the many gifts that come with the territory.

What Can We Learn?

What can we learn from the siblings who shared their stories? We can learn that every family has a story, because every family is on its own journey. And we can also learn that every sibling pair is on their own odyssey. When a sibling has ASD, it can be a true odyssey – a long and difficult trip filled with tumult, upheaval, and intensity.

The siblings we spoke to did not paint a Pollyannaish view of life with a sibling with ASD. They had to discard their expectations of what the sibling bond means, and forge a relationship with their brother or sister in their own way.

No one chooses to be a sibling of a person with ASD. However, as our interviewees attest, those who do find themselves in this extraordinary role can find meaning, inspiration, and happiness in their families, for themselves, and in relationships with their special siblings.

Appendix A: Future Planning Ideas

Planning for the future of a person with a disability is an enormously complex and challenging prospect. Discussing the subject can be unpleasant, as it involves the basic fact that one day, parents will no longer be able to take care of their special child's needs. Nevertheless, it is essential that siblings encourage their parents to make future plans and that they themselves get involved in these efforts.

The first step is to talk about everyone's expectations for the future. Typical siblings need to understand what is involved in their special sibling's care and must be willing to take on this responsibility, if that is the plan. The following information, while not exhaustive, represents some of the "current wisdom" and is intended to serve as a roadmap for future planning. Because individual needs vary greatly from family to family, not all of the issues presented here are applicable or necessary for everyone. The process of planning for the future takes time and depends, sometimes, on parents' motivation level or state of well-being. In any event, taking some of the measures discussed below will, at the very least, strengthen a family and sibling's abilities to face the future with greater confidence and peace of mind.

1. Meet with a Qualified Lawyer

Laws affecting people with disabilities are constantly changing and vary from state to state. Families should retain a lawyer whose expertise is disability law and who has a lot of experience writing wills and trusts for families that include a person with a disability.

Such lawyers may be found in several ways. The best approach is to ask other local parents or siblings of individuals with special needs for a referral. Another way to access information from other families is through Internet discussion groups such as the one hosted by the Special Needs Advocate for Parents (S.N.A.P.) community (www.snap-info.org). Local chapters of national disability advocacy groups, such as the Autism Society of America (www.autism-society.org) or the Arc of the United States (www.thearc.org), are helpful sources for names of expert lawyers. Similarly, an attorney may be found through (a) regional advocacy groups such as The New Jersey Center for Outreach and Services for the Autism Community (www.njcosac.org), (b) professional associations such as the National Academy of Elder Attorneys (www.naela.org), or (c) local bar associations.

2. Perform Estate Planning

Parents should be encouraged to establish and keep an updated will. Without one, the death of a parent can destabilize the financial well-being of a family, and a dependent with disabilities in particular. This is true because the estate of someone who dies without a will might go in unintended directions and assets might be frozen for a significant length of time. A properly prepared will, on the other hand, can (a) let others know how parents want things distributed and (b) name a guardian for a child with a disability.

Special needs trust. A crucial point that many people miss is that a direct gift or an inheritance of more than $2,000 to a person with a disability may cause disqualification from most state and federal governmental assistance programs, including Supplemental Security Income and Medicaid. Moreover, in some states a direct bequest will expose assets to recoupment statutes regarding services rendered in the past. A special needs trust, which holds title to property for the benefit of a person with a disability, is a way of providing financial support and basic maintenance for a loved one while keeping him or her eligible for public benefits.

A trust is a legal entity that is governed by state law and should be drafted by an attorney. The special needs trust allows a parent to give assets to a trustee (say, a typically developing sibling) with directions that they be used for the benefit of a third-party beneficiary (child with disability). Special needs trusts usually provide for transportation expenses, education, insurance, and personal services, among many others. It can be an effective mechanism for managing the affairs of a person with a disability.

The trust can be funded with different types of assets, including personal property, art, investments, and insurance policy proceeds. Relatives can also be encouraged to give to the trust for the benefit of the child with a disability. The trust can go into effect either while parents are alive or after their deaths.

Pooled trust funds. Another way of providing funds for an individual with a disability without jeopardizing any entitlements to public benefits is through a pooled trust program. Here, a family establishes a trust account (or "subaccount") with an established trust program managed by a nonprofit organization. The program combines these funds with those of other subaccounts and invests the money as one account.

Theoretically, a pooled trust fund may provide a greater rate of return for families, who typically are entitled to earnings based on their share of the principal. *Nevertheless, pooled trust funds vary greatly, and families must carefully investigate the parameters of any program they are considering.* Anyone interested in this type of trust should read "Pooled Trust Programs for People with Disabilities: A Guide for Families," an informative guide published recently by the Arc of the United States. The publication, which includes a list of at least 30 pooled trust programs, may be downloaded for free from the resources section of the organization's website, www.thearc.org.

The information discussed in an estate planning consultation can overwhelm even the most educated family members. Thus, it is a good idea to become familiar with some basic terms pertaining to wills, trusts, and benefits before the appointment with an attorney. This will not only make a discussion with the attorney more manageable, it will help family members formulate their questions before or during the meeting – instead of two days later! A good starting point is the attorney's office, which may distribute pamphlets or other literature to clients seeking estate planning services for their loved ones with disabilities. Also, various Internet sites provide background information on estate planning for people with disabilities. A good one is the estate planning section of the Family Village website, www.familyvillage.wisc.edu/general/estate.htm.

3. Determine Whether Guardianship/Conservatorship Is Appropriate

A family's discussion of the future is incomplete without deciding whether establishing a guardianship or a conservatorship is appropriate for the person with ASD. These statutory mechanisms are defined differently from state to state, but generally grant an adult the legal right to make decisions for another person. Such decisions relate to important areas of a person's life, including medical treatment, housing arrangements, and use of financial resources. Therefore, family members should carefully analyze whether to appoint a guardian or a conservator.

In cases where a person is fairly incapacitated by a disability, the decision to appoint a guardian or conservator is obvious. Where this is not the case, families should ask whether, among other things, the person with ASD can (a) make decisions about common day-to-day activities; (b) take safety precautions at home or in public; (c) make responsible financial decisions and recognize whether he or she is being cheated; (d) comply with treatment regimes, including prescribed medication; and (e) understand legal contracts, such as housing or car leasing agreements. Depending on the nature and severity of a person's disability, he or she may be fully capable of managing some of these decisions and may wish to preserve his or her independence. In such cases, a limited guardianship or conservatorship might be the answer. This would allow the person with a disability to, say, make health care decisions, but would let a limited guardian or conservator handle other important issues.

Parents typically fulfill the guardianship role during their lifetimes. If it is decided that a typical sibling will act as conservator or guardian for a brother or sister after the parents die, the sibling should be named as the successor guardian in the parents' will. Since the sibling's competency to fulfill this role must be approved by a court, an expert attorney should be hired to represent the family in establishing the guardianship or conservatorship.

4. Decide Where the Person with ASD Will Live

It may be difficult for a typical sibling to discuss this issue with parents, but whether that sibling intends to ever live with a brother or sister with ASD is a question that needs to be addressed honestly and straightforwardly. Typical siblings need to first determine what their true feelings are on this issue, taking into account their own immediate family situations and resources. In some situations, a long-term living arrangement is already in place that is not expected to change. In other cases, an adult child is still living in the family home with aging parents, who are either (a) unable to arrange a comfortable housing solution for the future, or (b) unwilling to talk about the whole subject. And that is where special planning comes in.

A typical sibling might open the topic for discussion by taking the lead on getting information, perhaps by attending a seminar or workshop. He or she might then share the brochures or handouts from such an event, and ask the parents to review them.

Sometimes, siblings ask a parent to join them either in attending such a workshop or in making a personal visit to an attorney's office. Some siblings have enlisted the help of others in the family to speak separately or together with their parents. For example, a trusted aunt or uncle or a parent's close friend might be able to support a parent through the early stages of addressing these issues. Occasionally, a visit to a professional mediator such as a therapist might help the family to address the issues more directly and effectively.

Every state has its own policies regarding eligibility for services. Therefore, families must acquaint themselves with the relevant procedures well before the individual with ASD becomes an adult. First of all, it is important that the individual is deemed eligible, and is placed on appropriate waiting lists, which can be extremely long. Many families are lulled into a sense of security during the school-age years, where intervention is secure, and is a legal entitlement. There is more competition for limited resources at the adult level, and the strong mandate for educational intervention ends at age 21.

Some families choose to carefully construct a placement, but that is not easy. For example, they may decide to purchase a group home along with other interested families. They may try to work with the educational or vocational service provider to encourage that agency to begin a residential program or to add a new home. Sometimes these arrangements are fruitful, but they are often very complicated both logistically and financially. Moreover, family members might be forced to take on multiple or dual roles, as they continue in the role of family member but now also function as a program founder. It is easier if, by the onset of adulthood, the individual with ASD is already residentially placed or served by an educational program with adult vocational and residential programs.

In any case, families must always work with the appropriate state services agency to ensure that funding sources will be available. Families who operate independent of these agencies will find that service providers are confused by a subsequent inquiry into placements. The providers will wonder, for example, whether the state or the family is funding the placement. Given the paucity of public funding and changing political climates, it is best to be both working with the state agency in charge of such decisions and allocations and privately advocating and searching for residential options.

Living arrangements for persons with ASD vary along a continuum from supervised apartments in the community, to community-based group homes, to residential care facilities that may be located in more of a campus-like setting. A number of factors determine which of these placements is best for a given individual, including behavioral characteristics and levels of independence and self-sufficiency. It is a good idea to visit several such settings to get a sense of how they differ and what would constitute a good fit for an individual.

5. "Know Thy Sibling and Parents"

Siblings don't typically pry into the minute details of their brothers' or sisters' lives. However, when a brother or sister has a disability, obtaining additional information can enable a typical sibling to step in if this is ever required. As such, it is helpful for a typical sibling to

gather or have access to personal information regarding their sibling with ASD. Possible topics could include the sibling's:
- complete medical history
- medication requirements, including any side effects or previous reactions
- contact information for doctors and other service providers
- health and hygiene regime
- insurance policies, including policy numbers
- Social Security number
- administrative requirements for public benefits, if applicable
- assets, debts, and contractual obligations
- strong likes or dislikes
- communication modality, including anything unusual about how he or she communicates
- challenging behaviors, past and present
- skill sets
- address and phone number
- case manager's name and contact information for any state agency currently providing services

Similarly, it is helpful to know certain information about your parents, if they are agreeable to divulging such details. For instance, a typical sibling could find out:
- where parents keep their will (or get a copy of it)
- what their assets are (including account numbers), and where the documentation is kept
- where insurance policies are kept, especially as they relate to future financial arrangements for the sibling with a ASD
- how to find the deed to the parents' house
- the names of lawyers, accountants, and other professionals the parents have retained regarding their estate
- location of and key to family's safe deposit box

Appendix B:
How to Explain ASD
to Others

In the life of a family member of a person with ASD, explaining the disorder becomes necessary at times. In part, this is because ASD is an invisible disability. It is hard to come up with descriptors of ASD that are true to its nature, that cover the disability adequately, and that are comprehensible to those who do not encounter it regularly.

The most important explanations are ones made to children, peers, and community members.

Explaining Autism to Children

There are many circumstances in which a family member has to offer an explanation to children. For example, parents of a child with ASD and a typically developing youngster will need to explain ASD to the typical child. They will also likely have to explain it to the typical child's peers as well as to children on the block or in the family's place of worship. Additionally, adult siblings of a person with ASD may need to explain the disability to their own children. It is especially important for siblings to find a way to convey to their children the love and affection that exist for the family member with ASD, and to facilitate ways for children to successfully interact with their aunt or uncle. It is not always necessary to say anything, especially when the child is young. If an explanation is needed, it can be kept short and centered on preparing the child for some of the things that may be confusing.

Uncle Joey will be so happy to see you! Sometimes it is hard to understand what he says, because he has trouble talking clearly. I'll help you understand him if you can't hear what he says. He really likes to go to McDonald's so we'll have lunch together there, and then you can play in the playroom. You might want to bring your picture from school; he loves rainbows!

How ASD gets explained to a child depends in large part on the child's developmental level. In general, a very young child may be given the simplest of explanations. Themes to cover include that the child with autism has not yet learned to talk (or perform other skills), and that the parents will ensure the safety of the typical child. This is especially important if there are frightening challenging behaviors. For example:

Joey is learning to talk; it is hard for him. We're working hard to help him learn to talk.

I will make sure you are safe; that he doesn't hurt you.

By the age of 6 or 7, children may be developing their own erroneous explanations and should be provided with reassurance. For example, they may fear that ASD is contagious or that their brother got the disorder as a punishment for misbehavior. It is especially important to address possible fears of catching ASD. It may also be helpful to make it clear that it is not anyone's fault that ASD is in the family.

Remember when we visited Max and Sam? I asked Max about his brother's autism that day. Max told me that his brother got autism from a bad cold. Then his mom explained that you can't get autism from a cold, and that autism isn't a sickness you can catch.

Autism just happens sometimes. He didn't do anything wrong, and neither did anyone else. It isn't going to happen to you; it only happens when people are tiny babies.

An older child (9 or 10 years old) can understand much more about the nature of ASD.

Autism is a problem in the brain. It happens very early in life, usually before the person is born. Autism makes it hard for your brother to do a lot of things. He can learn, but it takes a lot of work for him.

Children of this age may also have concerns about talking to friends, and about what their role should be regarding their sibling with ASD. It is important for parents to make themselves available for discussions about any related issues, especially about talking to friends. Parents should also be explicit about helping a typical child find a comfortable role. This is a delicate matter. Certainly, children should never be forced to assume any role with their sibling with ASD. However, many siblings are unsure of how to interact with or be helpful to their brother or sister with autism, and would welcome guidance in this respect. Parents can suggest methods for playing with the sibling, and for choosing activities that will likely proceed well. Furthermore, parents should clearly state that a sibling is not expected to intervene in dangerous behavioral escalations, but rely on their parents to handle such situations.

You might want to watch "Dragon Tales" with Joshua. He loves the middle part when everyone gets up to sing and dance. That would be a fun thing to do with him!

If you want to teach Kate how to play baseball, we can do it together. Tell her to watch you while you hold the bat, and have her copy you. Then, when it's her turn to hit the ball, say "Get ready" and "Look at me." Then, throw her the ball. Make sure you cheer for her. Even if she doesn't hit the ball, we can cheer her for trying!

Listen, if you run into trouble with Kevin, let me know. If he gets upset or hits you, just come get me or call for me. You don't need to calm him down; that's my job.

For a more complete description of how to tailor explanations to a child's age and level of understanding, readers should consult *Siblings of Children with Autism: A Guide for Families* (Woodbine House, 2003) by Sandra L. Harris and Beth Glasberg.

Explaining ASD to Peers

Typical siblings need to find a way to explain the behaviors and characteristics of their brother or sister with ASD to friends. It is important for parents to assist with this process. Autism is difficult even for adults to explain, and most children are quite befuddled when trying to figure out how to convey its nature. Often, it is understood by a child in terms of what it is *not* (i.e., he is not retarded). It is much harder to describe it in terms of what it *is* (a developmental disorder). Even when children know and use the label "autism," they do not always understand what it means. They may even have a few pat descriptors, but not be able to answer questions about it. They may simply be echoing what they have heard and be able to reiterate it, but not to explain it.

Just as in tailoring explanations to a child within the family, explanations offered to any other child must match his or her level of general comprehension. The guidelines above can be used as a framework.

Other special issues to attend to with peers might include the following.

Contagiousness

In this context, it is most important to quell any fears of contagion. It should be specifically stated that ASD cannot be caught, that it is not an illness like a virus. For example, typical siblings could explain to peers that:

> He has autism. You can't catch it or anything like that. He was born with it, and it makes him different.

Fear of the Behaviors of the Person with ASD

Children may not express this fear. However, if they have observed frightening behaviors, reassurance can be provided.

> My mom will be with Matt in the kitchen while we play in the playroom. He never really tantrums at home, but if he does, my mom can calm him down really fast.

Emphasis on Everyone's Similarities

Often, when encountering ASD for the first time, the similarities between people with ASD and the rest of us are obscured. Like all of us, individuals with ASD have preferences, interests, and skills they are exceptional at. It often helps typical siblings to communicate some of those things.

> *There are a lot of things he can't do or that seem weird, but there's also a lot of regular things and cool things about him. Just like us, he likes "Rescue Heroes" and cowboy stuff. He is even better than me at reading, even though he hardly talks. And he can play baseball as well as I can.*

Skill Sets

Some siblings want their friends to know that their brother or sister with ASD is not faking it or deliberately not doing things. The variability that characterizes ASD sometimes creates false impressions about the purposefulness of such skill demonstration.

> *Stuff is just really hard for her. Some days she can do it, and then some days she can't. It took me a while to realize that. She isn't just pretending not to hear you or ignoring you. Sometimes she can pay attention, and sometimes she can't.*

Explaining ASD to a Potential Mate or Partner

Adult siblings will have to explain their brother or sister's ASD to most people, especially potential romantic partners. For newer dating relationships, it is important to address issues such as the presence of the person in the family and how it impacts the individual. For a spouse, additional issues come up regarding level of involvement and responsibility as well as the choice of whether to have children. Possible approaches include the following:

I just want you to know that I have a brother with autism. I don't want to keep it from you. He's a big part of my life. Most people are a little intimidated at first, because they don't know what autism means or how to act around him. If we get to that point, I'll help you know what to do. He's really pretty cool, very different from you and me, but a neat person.

We need to talk about what happens after my parents can't care for Roger any more. You know that I feel obligated to make sure he is okay, but I also want to make sure that we only do what we are both comfortable with. Things we need to think about are living arrangements, legal guardianship, and, generally, level of involvement.

I am terrified of having a kid with a disability because of Ben. I know you are probably scared, too. I think we should meet with a genetics counselor, just to learn more about it and help us figure out how we feel about it all.

Explaining ASD to People in the Community

At times, an explanation must be offered to someone in the community with whom one does not have an ongoing relationship. This often occurs in the context of a behavioral escalation, which may have frightened or alarmed those nearby. It is not easy in these circumstances to provide an adequate explanation, especially since one's attention must be fully focused on the person with ASD. However, it is sometimes helpful and occasionally necessary to provide a brief description.

I just want to tell you that he has autism. Sometimes he gets really overwhelmed when we go out into the community. We are working to help him be able to do these kinds of things, but today it was too much for him. Thank you for your offer to help, but he will calm down faster if he is surrounded by his family and people he knows well.

He has autism, which makes it hard for him to understand and communicate, and sometimes it results in these kinds of behaviors. I need to help him right now, so I won't be able to continue to chat about it. Thank you for your concern, and sorry for the disturbance.

Appendix C: Resources

Support Groups

The Sibling Support Project, The Arc of the United States
6512 23rd Avenue NW, Suite 213
Seattle, WA 98117
(206) 297-636
www.thearc.org/siblingsupport
(site contains a complete list of sibling support groups throughout the country);
to subscribe to online listservs, go to www.thearc.org/siblingsupport/sibkids.htm
and www.thearc.org/siblingsupport/sibnet.htm

Organizations

The Arc of the United States
1010 Wayne Avenue, Suite 650
Silver Spring, MD 20910
(301) 565-3842
www.thearc.org

Maap Services, Inc.
P.O. Box 524
Crown Point, IN 46308
(219) 662-1311
www.maapservices.org

Autism Research Institute
4182 Adams Avenue
San Diego, CA 92116
(619) 281-7165
www.autism.com/ari/

Autism Society of America
7910 Woodmont Avenue, Suite 300
Bethesda, MD 20814
(800) 3 AUTISM
www.autism-society.org

Center for the Study of Autism
P.O. Box 4538
Salem, OR 97302
www.autism.org

Cure Autism Now Foundation
5455 Wilshire Boulevard, Suite 715
Los Angeles, CA 90036-4234
(888) 8 AUTISM
www.cureautismnow.org

Indiana Resource Center for Autism (IRCA)
Indiana Institute on Disability and Community
2853 E. Tenth Street
Bloomington, IN 47408-2696
(812) 855-6508
www.iidc.indiana.edu/irca

National Alliance for Autism Research
99 Wall Street, Research Park
Princeton, NJ 08540
(888) 777-NAAR
www.naar.org

National Association of Protection and Advocacy Systems, Inc.
900 2nd Street NE, Suite 211
Washington, DC 20002
(202) 408-9514
www.napas.org

National Dissemination Center for Children with Disabilities
P.O. Box 1492
Washington, DC 20013
(800) 695-0285
www.nichcy.org

The New Jersey Center for Outreach and Services for the Autism Community
1450 Parkside Avenue, Suite 22
Ewing, NJ 08638
(609) 883-8100
www.njcosac.org

Parents Helping Parents
3041 Olcott Street
Santa Clara, CA 95054
(408) 727-5775
www.php.com

Siblings for Significant Change
350 Fifth Avenue, Suite 627
New York, NY 10118
(800) 841-8251

Treatment and Education of Autistic and related Communication handicapped
Children (Division TEACCH)
Administration and Research
The University of North Carolina at Chapel Hill, CB #7180
Chapel Hill, NC 27599-6305
(919) 966-2174
www.teacch.com

Books

Barron, J., & Barron, S. *There's a Boy in Here*. Simon & Schuster, 1992.

Carter, R. *Helping Someone with Mental Illness: A Compassionate Guide for Family, Friends, and Caregivers*. Random House, 1998.

Gartenberg, Z. *Mori's Story: A Book About a Boy with Autism*. Lerner Publications Co., 1998.

Grandin, T. *Emergence: Labeled Autistic*. Warner, 1996.

Grandin, T. *Thinking in Pictures*. Vintage, 1996.

Harris, S. L., & Glasberg, B. A. *Siblings of Children with Autism: A Guide for Families*. Woodbine House, 2003.

Lears, L. *Ian's Walk: A Story About Autism*. Albert Whitman & Co., 1998.

Leonard-Toomey, P. *In Our Own Words: Stories by Brothers and Sisters of Children with Autism and P.D.D.* Adsum, Inc., 1997.

Lerner, H. *The Dance of Anger: A Woman's Guide to Changing the Patterns of Intimate Relationships.* Quill, 1997.

Lobato, D. J. *Brothers, Sisters, and Special Needs: Information and Activities for Helping Young Siblings of Children with Chronic Illnesses and Developmental Disabilities.* Paul H. Brookes Publishing Co., 1990.

Maurice, C. *Let Me Hear Your Voice: A Family's Triumph over Autism.* Knopf, 1993.

McHugh, M. *Special Siblings*. Paul H. Brookes Publishing Co., 2003.

Meyer, D. *Views from Our Shoes*. Woodbine House, 1997.

Powers, M. D. *Children with Autism: A Parents' Guide*. Woodbine House, 2nd ed., 2000.

Rosenberg, M. S. *Coping When a Brother or Sister is Autistic*. Rosen Publishing Group, 2001.

Remen, N. R. *Kitchen Table Wisdom*. Riverhead Books, 1996.

Simon, R. *Riding the Bus with My Sister: A True Life Journey*. Houghton Mifflin Co., 2002.

Thompson, M. *Andy and His Yellow Frisbee*. Woodbine House, 1996.

Williams, D. *Nobody Nowhere*. Avon, 1994.

Other Publications

Autism Research Review International newsletter
Autism Research Institute
4182 Adams Avenue
San Diego, CA 92116
(619) 281-7165
ww.autismresearchinstitute.com

Exceptional Parent magazine
P.O. Box 2079
Marion, OH 43306
(877) 372-7368
www.exceptionalparent.com

Families magazine
New Jersey Council on Developmental Disabilities
P.O. Box 700
Trenton, NJ 08625-0700
(609) 292-3745
www.njddc.org

IRCA Reporter newsletter
Indiana Resource Center for Autism
2853 E. Tenth Street
Bloomington, IN 47408-2696
(812) 855-6508
www.iidc.indiana.edu/irca/newsletter1.html

News Digest
National Dissemination Center for Children and Youth with Disabilities
P.O. Box 1492
Washington, DC 20013
(800) 695-0285
www.nichcy.org

The Pacesetter newsletter
Parent Advocacy Coalition for Educational Rights
8161 Normandale Blvd.
Minneapolis, MN 55437
(952) 838-9000
www.pacer.org

Sibling Forum (ages 10 and up) and *For Siblings Only* (ages 4-10) newsletters
Family Resource Associates
35 Haddon Avenue
Shrewsbury, NJ 07702
(732) 747-5310

Videotapes

Asperger Syndrome: Transition to College & Work
Coulter Video
www.coultervideo.com

Brothers and Sisters
Autism Society of British Columbia
301-3701 East Hastings Street
Burnaby, BC Canada V5C2H6
(888) 437-0880
www.autismbc.ca/

Day by Day: Raising the Child with Autism/PDD
Guilford Publications
72 Spring Street
New York, NY 10012
(800) 365-7006
www.guilford.com

Refrigerator Mothers
Fanlight Productions
4196 Washington Street
Boston, MA 02131
(800) 937-4113
www.fanlight.com

Starting a Group Home from Scratch
Autism Services Center Films
www.autismservicescenter.org

What About Me?
Educational Productions
9000 Southwest Gemini Drive
Beaverton, OR 97008
(800) 950-4949
www.edpro.com

Benefits

To learn about eligibility for Supplemental Security Income or to apply for Medicare, call the Social Security Administration at (800) 772-1213, or go to http://www.ssa.gov/.

Miscellaneous Websites

National Institute of Child Health and Human Development Autism Web Page, www.nichd.nih.gov/autism

Special Needs Advocate for Parents, www.snapinfo.org

Future Planning

Certified Financial Planner Board of Standards
1700 Broadway, Suite 2100
Denver, CO 80290
(888) CFP-MARK
www.CFP-Board.org

Financial Planning Association
1615 L Street NW, Suite 650
Washington, DC 20036
(800) 322-4237
www.fpanet.org

National Academy of Elder Law Attorneys, Inc.
1604 North Country Club Road
Tucson, AZ 85716
(520) 881-4005
www.naela.org

With Open Arms: Embracing a Bright Financial Future for You and Your Child
Open Arms/Easter Seals
230 W. Monroe, Suite 1800
Chicago, IL 60606
(To order a printed copy of this booklet, send a $5 check payable to Easter Seals to above address; a downloadable copy of the booklet is available through the organization's website at www.easter-seals.org)

References

Abramovich, R., Stanhope, L., Pepler, D., & Corter, C. (1987). The influence of Down's syndrome in sibling interaction. *Journal of Consulting and Clinical Psychology, 28,* 865-879.

Albanese, A. L., San Miguel, S. K., & Koegel, R. L. (1996). Social support for families. In R. L. Koegel & L. K. Koegel (Eds.), *Teaching children with autism: Strategies for initiating positive interactions and improving learning opportunities* (pp. 95-104). Baltimore: Paul H. Brookes.

Bank, S. P., & Kahn, M. D. (1982). *The sibling bond.* New York: Basic Books.

Bouma, R., & Schweitzer, R. (1990). The impact of chronic childhood illness on family stress: A comparison between autism and cystic fibrosis. *Journal of Clinical Psychology, 46,* 722-730.

Boyce, G., Behl, D., Mortensen, L., & Akers, J. (1991). Child characteristics, demographics, and family processes: Their effects on the stress experienced by families of children with disabilities. *Counseling Psychology Quarterly, 4,* 273-288.

Boyce, G. C., & Barnett, W. S. (1993). Siblings of persons with mental retardation: A historical perspective and recent findings. In Z. Stoneman & P. W. Berman (Eds.), *The effects of mental retardation, disability, & illness on sibling relationships: Research issues and challenges* (pp. 145-184). Baltimore: Paul H. Brookes.

Bristol, M. M. (1985). Designing programs for young developmentally disabled children: A family systems approach to autism. *RASE, 6,* 46-53.

Bristol, M. M. (1986). The home care of developmentally disabled children: Empirical support for a model of successful family coping with stress. In S. Landesman-Dwyer & P. Vietze (Eds.), *Living with mentally retarded persons* (pp. 120-146). Washington, DC: American Association of Mental Deficiency.

Bristol, M. M., & Schopler, E. (1983). Stress and coping in families of autistic adolescents. In E. Schopler & G. B. Mesibov (Eds.), *Autism in adolescents and
adults* (pp. 251-278). New York: Plenum.

Brody, G. H., Stoneman, Z., Davis, C. H., & Crapps, J. M. (1991). Observations of
the role relations and behavior between older children with mental retardation and their younger siblings. *American Journal of Mental Retardation,
95*, 527-536.

Brodzinsky, D. M., Pappas, C., Singer, L. M., & Braff, A. M. (1981). Children's conception of adoption: A preliminary investigation. *Journal of Pediatric
Psychology, 6,* 177-189.

Brodzinsky, D. M., Schechter, D., & Brodzinsky, A. B. (1986). Children's knowledge
of adoption: Developmental changes and implications for adjustment. In R.
D. Ashmore & D. M. Brodzinsky (Eds.), *Thinking about the family: Views of
parents and children* (pp. 205-232.) Hillsdale, NJ: Erlbaum.

Buhrmester, D. (1992). The developmental courses of sibling peer relationships.
In F. Boer & J. Dunn (Eds.), *Children's sibling relationships: Developmental and
clinical issues* (pp. 19-40). Hillsdale, NJ: Erlbaum.

Byrne, E. A., & Cunningham, C. C. (1985). The effects of mentally handicapped
children on families: A conceptual review. *Journal of Child Psychology and
Psychiatry, 26,* 847-864.

Cicirelli, V. G. (1995). *Sibling relationships across the life span.* New York: Plenum Press.

Cohen, F., & Lazarus, R. (1979). Coping with the stress of illness. In G. C. Stone
& N. Adler (Eds.), *Health psychology: A handbook* (pp. 140-168). San
Francisco: Jossey-Bass.

Donovan, A. M. (1988). Family stress and ways of coping with adolescents who
have handicaps: Maternal perceptions. *American Journal on Mental Retardation,
92,* 502-509.

Dunn, J. (1992). Introduction. In F. Boer & J. Dunn (Eds.), *Children's sibling relationships: Developmental and clinical issues* (pp. xiii-xv). Hillsdale, NJ: Erlbaum.

Dyson, L., Edgar, E., & Crnic, K. (1989). Psychological predictors of adjustment
by siblings of developmentally disabled children. *American Journal of Mental
Retardation, 94,* 292-302.

Dyson, L. L. (1989). Adjustment of siblings of handicapped children: A comparison. *Journal of Pediatric Psychology, 14*, 215-229.

Farran, D. C., & Sparling, J. (1988). Coping styles in families of handicapped children. In E. D. Hibbs (Ed.), *Children and families: Studies in prevention and intervention* (pp. 351-366). Madison, CT: International Universities Press.

Gamble, W. C., & Woulbroun, E. J. (1993). Measurement considerations in the identification and assessment of stressors and coping strategies. In Z. Stoneman & P. W. Berman (Eds.), *The effects of mental retardation, disability, and illness on sibling relationships: Research issues and challenges* (pp. 287-319). Baltimore: Paul H. Brookes.

Glasberg, B. (2000). The development of siblings' understanding of autism spectrum disorders. *Journal of Autism and Developmental Disorders, 30,* 143-156.

Gold, N. (1993). Depression and social adjustment in siblings of boys with autism. *Journal of Autism and Developmental Disorders, 23,* 147-163.

Grissom, M., & Borkowski, J. G. (2002). Self-efficacy in adolescents who have siblings with or without disabilities. *American Journal of Mental Retardation, 107,* 79-90.

Grossman, F. K. (1972). *Brothers and sisters of retarded children: An exploratory study.* Syracuse, NY: Syracuse University Press.

Harris, S. L. (1983). *Families of the developmentally disabled: A guide to behavioral intervention.* Elmsford, NY: Pergamon Press.

Harris, S. L. (1984). The family and the autistic child: A behavioral perspective. *Family Practice, 33,* 127-134.

Harris, S. L., & Glasberg, B. (2003). *Siblings of children with autism: A guide for families.* Bethesda, MD: Woodbine House.

Honig, A. S., & Winger, C. J. (1997). A professional support program for families of handicapped preschoolers: Decrease in maternal stress. *The Journal of Primary Prevention, 17,* 285-296.

Johnson, J. H., & Sarason, I. G. (1978). Life stress, depression, and anxiety: Internal-external control as a moderator variable. *Journal of Psychosomatic Research, 22,* 205-208.

Kaminsky, L., & Dewey, D. (2001). Sibling relationships of children with autism. *Journal of Autism and Developmental Disorders, 31,* 399-410.

Kazak, A. E., & Marvin, R. S. (1984). Differences, difficulties, and adaptation: Stress and social networks in families with a handicapped child. *Family Relations, 33,* 67-77.

Koegel, R. L., Schreibman, L., Loos, L. M., Dirlich-Wilhelm, H., Dunlap, G., Robbins, F. R., & Plienis, A. J. (1992). Consistent stress profiles in mothers of children with autism. *Journal of Autism and Developmental Disorders, 22,* 205-216.

Lazarus, R., & Folkman, S. (1984). *Stress, appraisal, and coping.* New York: Springer.

Leder, J. M. (1991). *Brothers & sisters: How they shape our lives.* New York: St. Martin's Press.

Lobato, D. J. (1983). Siblings of handicapped children: A review. *Journal of Autism and Developmental Disorders, 13,* 347-364.

Lobato, D. J. (1990). *Brothers, sisters, and special needs.* Baltimore: Paul H. Brookes.

Lobato, D. J., Faust, D., & Spirato, S. (1988). Examining the effects of chronic disease and disability on children's sibling relationships. *Journal of Pediatric Psychology, 13,* 389-407.

Marsh, D. T. (1993). *Families and mental retardation.* New York: Praeger.

McCubbin, H. (1979). Integrating coping behavior in family stress theory. *Journal of Marriage and the Family, 41,* 237-244.

McHale, S., & Gamble, W. (1989). Sibling relationships of children with disabled and nondisabled brothers and sisters. *Developmental Psychology, 25,* 421-429.

McHale, S. M., & Gamble, W. C. (1987). Sibling relationships and the adjustment of children with disabled brothers. *Journal of Children in Contemporary Society, 19,* 131-158.

McHale, S., Sloan, J., & Simeonsson, R. (1986). Sibling relationships of children with autistic, mentally retarded, and non-handicapped brothers and sisters. *Journal of Autism and Mental Disorders, 16,* 399-413.

Merrell, S. S. (1995). *The accidental bond: How sibling connections influence adult relationships.* New York: Fawcett Columbine.

Moes, D., Koegel, R. L., Schreibman, L., & Loos, L. M. (1992). Stress profiles for mothers and fathers of children with autism. *Psychological Reports, 71,* 1272-1274.

O'Kane Grissom, M., & Borkowski, J. G. (2002). Self-efficacy in adolescents who have siblings with or without disabilities. *American Journal on Mental Retardation, 107,* 79-90.

Rodrigue, J. R., Geffken, G. R., & Morgan, S. B. (1993). Perceived competence and behavioral adjustment of siblings of children with autism. *Journal of Autism and Developmental Disorders, 23,* 665-674.

Rodrigue, J. R., Morgan, S. B., & Geffken, G. (1990). Families of autistic children: Psychosocial functioning of mothers. *Journal of Clinical Child Psychology, 19,* 371-379.

Seligman, M., & Darling, R. B. (1997). *Ordinary families, special children.* New York: Guilford.

Seligman, M.E.P. (1991). *Learned optimism.* New York: Knopf.

Siegel, B., & Silverstein, S. (1994). *What about me? Growing up with a developmentally disabled sibling.* New York: Plenum.

Simeonsson, R. J., & McHale, S. M. (1981). Research on handicapped children: Sibling relations. *Child: Care, Health, and Development, 7,* 153-171.

Stoneman, Z., Brody, G. H., Davis, C. H., & Crapps, J. M. (1987). Mentally retarded children & their older same-sex siblings: Naturalistic in-home observations. *American Journal of Mental Retardation, 92,* 290-298.

Stoneman, Z., Brody, G. H., Davis, C. H., & Crapps, J. M. (1988). Childcare responsibilities, peer relations, & sibling conflict: Older siblings of mentally retarded children. *American Journal of Mental Retardation, 93,* 174-183.

Turnbull, A. P., & Turnbull, H. R. (1990). *Families, professionals, and exceptionality* (2nd ed.). Columbus, OH: Merrill.

Wolf, L. C., Noh, S., Fisman, S. N., & Speechley, M. (1989). Psychological effects of parenting stress on parents of autistic children. *Journal of Autism and Developmental Disorders, 19,* 157-166.